NO FEAR SOCK KNITTING

NO FEAR SOCK KNITTING

Take the worry out of knitting socks with this beginner's guide

Denise DeSantis

DAVID & CHARLES
— PUBLISHING —

www.davidandcharles.com

CONTENTS

INTRODUCTION

Dear Knitters,

There are so many sock knitting books at the bookstore, at the library, at your local yarn shop, so why another one? Because this one is written by a sock knitter who remembers what it was like to be a beginner. I remember the struggle to understand a pattern, trying to decide what yarn and needles to use, not to mention what size to make.

When you start out, there are so many decisions and choices and options. Tons of options!! Top down, toe up, which heel, which toe? Then deciding on cast ons and bind (cast) offs. Some of you may not even know what "sock" yarn to buy. Is there such a thing as sock yarn or can you just use fingering weight yarn? Don't worry, we'll get to all of that.

This book is based on the No Fear Sock Knitting Class on my YouTube channel. My goal there and here is to provide you, the beginner (as well as experienced) sock knitter, with the information you need to build a foundation of understanding that eliminates fear and worry. Once you understand all of the moving parts of sock knitting, the fear will be gone and you can get on with the wonderful adventure that is sock knitting.

No Fear Sock Knitting is the book you never knew you always wanted, written by someone who, I hope, feels more like a friend than an expert doling out information.

So, my friends, it's time for some fearless sock knitting...

Love,

Denise

EarthtonesGirl

ABOUT THIS BOOK

I wish there were one book that contained everything there is to know about sock knitting but that is impossible. So, I offer you this book. It doesn't contain "The Way" to knit socks but MY WAY, the EarthtonesGirl way.

In these pages I will share not only my general knowledge, but also as many of my tips and tricks on sock knitting as I can. My goal is to help you achieve success and true satisfaction with YOUR sock knitting and remove all the learned fear that sock knitting is hard, complicated, and scary.

This book is divided into chapters containing all the basic information you will need to knit both top down and toe up socks. The answers to all of the frequently asked questions can be found in the chapters of this book, with the last chapter containing eight basic sock knitting patterns that utilize all of my favorite methods, techniques, tips, and tricks.

An opinion I've shared often, is that sock patterns are more like recipes or organized suggestions. You are the boss of your knitting. You are in control and if there is some thing you want to change, then change it. So this book contains a "Build Your Own Adventure" format, especially for working socks top down or toe up (see Knitting Up or Knitting Down).

Now, you can jump ahead to the patterns and start your sock knitting journey right away while referring to the necessary sections to look up a specific technique or refresh your memory.

Or, instead, you can start from the beginning, reading through the how and the why, then once you are ready and your bag of tricks is filled, cast on your first sock.

The choice is ultimately yours but whichever way you choose, I will be there guiding you every stitch along the way.

Now, let's start knitting!

KNITTING UP OR KNITTING DOWN?

I have often been asked whether socks should be knit down from the cuff, or up from the toe. When I hear this question two phrases come to mind, "Team Toe Up" and "Team Top Down". Until not too long ago I was a die-hard member of Team Top Down but I must confess that I now see the benefits to both methods, or rather "directions".

In my experience knitting socks from the top down made me a bit too comfortable. I had a formula, I cast on my stitches and the muscle memory took over. But two things happened: one, I got a bit lazy and forgot how much I love to experiment; and two, as a sock knitting teacher and designer I was neglecting an entire team of sock knitters, not to mention missing out on some amazing techniques.

Knitters seem to naturally gravitate to one team or the other, but once you've mastered the basics, I really encourage you to try both toe up and top down socks to discover the joy of going in both directions.

Throughout the book I've indicated which team a technique or pattern is primarily aimed at, using these symbols:

 for Team Top Down

 for Team Toe Up

To fully embrace both sides, Team Top Down and Team Toe Up, all of the patterns have guidelines to knit in either direction and interchange cuffs, heels, and toes. What does that mean? It means that while there are eight basic patterns, you have the option to cut and paste or change direction as you see fit.

CHAPTER ONE

Getting Started

"The expert in anything was once a beginner"

HELEN HAYES

What Do I Need To Knit Socks?

The answer is simple, two sticks and some string — but what kind of sticks and string can make a world of difference. Sock knitting, as with most things in life, requires experimenting to find what works best for you.

NEEDLES

Choosing a Type

When it comes to knitting needles, one size or type does not fit all. There are many brands and options to choose from. So, how do you know which one to choose? Experimentation and practice.

Circular needles and DPNs (double-pointed needles) are primarily used for sock knitting. Your preferred technique will determine which type of needle you use (see Methods: How Do I Manage Stitches on the Needles) and the needle size is determined by the gauge (tension) of your chosen sock pattern (see Planning: How Do I Read Patterns).

- DPNs: these come in sets of four or five needles. Some people prefer longer needles so the stitches are less likely to fall off. Others prefer shorter needles because it makes the transition from one needle to another a bit faster.
- Circular Needles: these are easier to use if the cable (cord) that runs between the needles is more flexible. Especially when knitting with the Magic Loop technique. If that cable is stiff the sock knitting experience can lead to unnecessary frustration. Circular needles come in different lengths, which you'll want to keep in mind when deciding which technique you're using to manage your stitches. An important thing to note is that the length measurement is the full length from one tip to the other, and not just the length of the cable between the tips.

The more common needle brands are Addi Rockets/Addi Sock Rockets, ChiaoGoo and HiyaHiya Sharps, Clover (bamboo), Knitter's Pride and Knit Picks, to name a few.

Choosing a Size

Fingering (4ply) weight socks generally require small needles ranging in diameter from US 0 (2mm) to US 2 (2.75mm). However, the size depends on the gauge (tension) required for a particular pattern (see Planning: How Do I Read Patterns). Some beginner sock knitters may find such tiny needles intimidating so I often suggest starting with a heaver weight yarn like DK (light worsted, see Yarn). This yarn weight is better suited to needles ranging from US 2–3 (3mm) to US 6 (4mm).

Finding the Perfect Pairing

There were so many moments over the years when I thought the problem was me, but it was the "needle pairing". Problems like split stitches, dropped stitches, and uneven stitches. To avoid these problems you need to find the perfect marriage between yarn and needle.

One element in pairing is the needle material, usually metal or wood. Metal needles provide a smoother feel which enables the stitches to move more freely on the needle. That is great if you like to knit close to the tip or "on the edge", but for a beginner that can sometimes feel like there is less control. Like the stitches are getting away from you. Wooden needles, including bamboo, have more friction, giving the knitter more control, a slower pace and very little chance of stitches falling off the needles (but it can happen, so be careful).

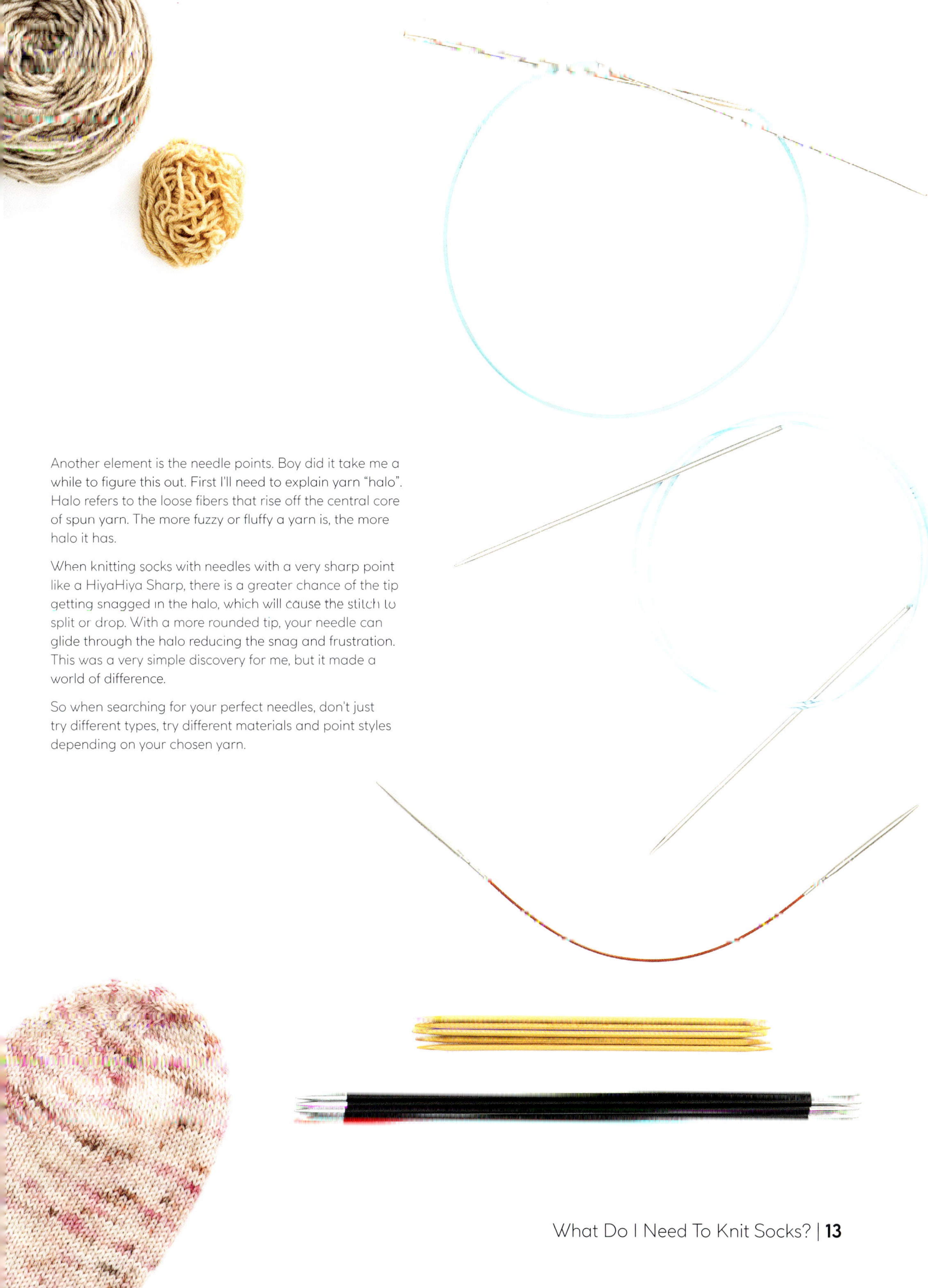

Another element is the needle points. Boy did it take me a while to figure this out. First I'll need to explain yarn "halo". Halo refers to the loose fibers that rise off the central core of spun yarn. The more fuzzy or fluffy a yarn is, the more halo it has.

When knitting socks with needles with a very sharp point like a HiyaHiya Sharp, there is a greater chance of the tip getting snagged in the halo, which will cause the stitch to split or drop. With a more rounded tip, your needle can glide through the halo reducing the snag and frustration. This was a very simple discovery for me, but it made a world of difference.

So when searching for your perfect needles, don't just try different types, try different materials and point styles depending on your chosen yarn.

YARN

Sock Yarn vs. Fingering (4ply) Weight Yarn

Socks can be knit in any weight yarn, from lace to super bulky. In general, most knitters lean towards using fingering (4ply) weight yarn with a percentage of nylon, a blend which is also often called "sock yarn". You can also use yarn with no nylon content (we'll get to that in Types of Fiber and Nylon versus No Nylon opposite).

Keep in mind that you don't need to start with fingering weight yarn at all. Socks knit in DK (light worsted) yarn use larger needles (see Needles), require less stitches, knit up much quicker, and enable the knitter to "see" the stitches a bit more clearer. That's why I've included the Fearless DK Socks (see Patterns), which is a great place to begin.

Commercial Yarn

Commercially dyed yarn is mass produced, has a wide, and in most cases, international distribution and has a lower price point. There are many brands producing commercial yarn — Knit Picks, Opal, Regia, Patons Kroy, West Yorkshire Spinners, John Arbon, to name a few. These brands produce yarns, including sock yarns, in different qualities with various fiber content, thicknesses, and characteristics. All sock yarns can produce beautiful, long lasting socks. Is one better than the other? Absolutely not, experiment with as many as you can to see which you prefer. I'm not responsible if you fall in love with all of them.

Commercial yarn is assigned two designators: a color name and/or number and a dye lot number. The dye lot number is given to a batch of yarn dyed at the same time. While the color name/number stays the same for each batch, the dye lot numbers change. This is only critical if you require more than one ball of yarn, and usually one 3½oz/100 gram ball is enough for a full pair of socks. For larger projects like knee-high socks or stockings or for those with large feet, you may need more yarn and then the dye lot number can be important so your socks match.

Indie/Hand Dyed Yarn

Indie/hand dyed yarn is produced by hand, in small batches, by small independent (indie) companies or artists. This type of yarn may be internationally or only locally available, usually has a higher price point, and colors can vary greatly from batch to batch. Some dyers specialize in different color distribution methods, such as tonal, speckles, variegated, and self-striping.

It would take pages and pages to name all of the indie dyers producing yarn, there are so many! There is a depth, richness, and variety to this type of yarn that makes it a very sought-after product. See Suppliers for a list of some of the hand dyed yarn I've used for the socks shown in this book.

So which should you knit with? Use as many different kinds of yarns and weights as you can. The most important thing is that you enjoy the sock knitting process, learn as much as you can, and have fun doing it.

Types of Fiber

Yarn fiber is another topic that could take pages and pages, and there are many books written on this topic. Yarns can be made all in one fiber or have a combination of fibers, whether natural or synthetic. But let's keep things simple.

In terms of natural fibers, the most commonly used base is sheep wool. And wool comes from many different breeds of sheep, such as Merino, Corriedale, Targhee and BFL (Bluefaced Leicester), to name a few. I have made socks from all of these wools and one is not better than another. The most obvious difference is the feel of the yarn once knit up. Merino tends to be softer to the touch while Corriedale and BFL might be categorized as workhorse yarns that create socks that are not necessarily as soft or texturally appealing, but your socks may last a little bit longer.

There are also other natural fibers that you may find in yarn, whether from other animals such as goats (cashmere or mohair), alpacas, llamas, and rabbits (angora), from plants such as cotton, bamboo, linen, and hemp, or even from insects (silk). These fibers have different characteristics (for example cashmere is soft with a fuzzy halo, cotton is very sturdy, and silk has amazing sheen) but these fibers are less often found in sock yarns. If they do appear it will often be in a blend with other fibers.

Synthetic fibers used in yarns include nylon, acrylic, and polyester. These fibers are manmade, and can be cheap and very durable. The one most commonly added to sock yarns is nylon.

Nylon versus No Nylon

No one knows the exact date knitting first came into being but from the very start all types of garments and accessories were made in 100% natural wool (in all its variations). Nylon, also known as polyamide, was not invented until 1935.

So do you need nylon in your sock yarn? That has been a debate for many years and there are very distinct camps on the subject. I have made socks with both a wool-nylon blend and 100% wool, and I love both.

Nylon provides reinforcement for the wool and delays the effects of normal day-to-day wear and tear. But you can combat that wear and tear in other ways too. One way is to be very mindful of your gauge (tension). The looser the gauge the easier it will be to wear out your socks, especially ones made without nylon. If your socks are knit at a tighter gauge, they will most certainly last longer.

Another way to add reinforcement when nylon is not present is to use textured stitch patterns. For example, slip stitch heel flaps are very popular because you are creating a double layer of fabric at a very high stress point in the sock. That added layer helps increase the longevity of your socks. I have also seen patterns that use slip stitches along the entire sole/bottom of the sock. Not only does it add that extra layer of durability, it also makes for a very squishy and super comfy sock.

NOTIONS

Notions are tools that knitters keep in their project bags to help facilitate the knitting process. These are just a few of the basics must-haves.

Stitch Markers

Stitch markers are essential to help keep your place in a pattern, mark off pattern repeats, hold stitches, and let you know how much progress you've made.

They come in many forms, including ring, bulb, split ring, and progress keepers, and in different materials like plastic or metal. They can also be decorative, like my progress keeper markers with motivational messages.

As you knit, stitch markers that are placed on the needles are "moving" with you. For example, bulb, ring, or split ring markers sit between stitches around the needle and are usually slipped from one needle to the other "when you come to them".

Other markers are intended to stay in the fabric of the sock until you move them yourself. Progress keepers have a clasp that opens and closes, so they can be clipped into a stitch on a particular row. I like to place a progress keeper every so often (such as every 10 rounds), or specifically to mark when I have worked an increase or decrease round. I can then use the marker to identify how many rounds I've completed, moving it when I have completed a section, or leave them in place so I can match the second sock.

Tapestry (Darning) Needle

A tapestry or darning needle is a larger-than-usual sewing needle and usually made of metal or plastic (though I have seen wooden ones too). They have a large eye in which yarn is threaded to finish off a sock. They are essential when grafting the toe closed, binding off a cuff, or weaving in ends. You can also use a tapestry needle to add in a lifeline.

Scissors/Thread Cutter

A small pair of folding scissors or a circular thread cutter is essential for cutting loose ends or cutting yarn from the ball/cake of yarn when your sock is complete. I absolutely suggest getting a pair of scissors that fold or a circular cutter because they are security friendly when traveling.

Ruler/Tape Measure

A small retractable tape measure or a bracelet ruler is a must have. This will allow you to quickly measure a portion of your sock and check your progress. Though you don't want to rely only on measuring tools... I do still recommend counting your rounds/rows and stitches for a perfectly matching pair of socks.

Scrap Yarn

Keeping a piece of scrap yarn, about 1–2yd/1–2m in your pouch is much more valuable than you may think. It can be used for a lifeline, provisional cast on, or to hold stitches if you need an extra needle or (gasp) lose a needle.

Handi Tool by Susan Bates

I consider this tool an absolutely essential notion and I never leave home without it. The versatile Handi Tool has a crochet hook on one end, a US 3 (3.25mm) knitting needle on the other, and a finger flat in the middle. I can honestly say I use this at least once in every project. The most common use for me is picking up stitches or fixing a split stitch, but it can also be used as a cable needle.

What Parts Make Up A Sock?

This information may seem obvious to some but when I first started knitting socks I had no idea what an instep was or why it was important. So let's briefly review the parts of a sock so we understand references to them throughout the book.

Cuff

The top part of the sock that grips the leg to keep it in place. It is often slightly narrower than the rest of the sock to help hold the sock on your leg. The narrowness is usually by design (using ribbing or other stitch patterns to make the fabric tighter) and not due to a change in stitch count (see Knitting Along: What Are My Cuff Options). For Team Top Down there are many cast on options to improve the stretchiness of the cuff for a good fit. For Team Toe Up, you want to be sure that your bind (cast) off is loose/flexible enough so the sock stretches over your foot but not too loose that the sock doesn't hold its shape and slides down.

Leg

The short or long tube portion of the sock that goes around the leg between the cuff and the ankle. This area can be plain stockinette (stocking stitch), or feature colorwork or a textured pattern.

Heel

The heel of a sock is what makes a sock! It is an L shaped pocket that fits snugly around the heel of your foot. The heel shape turns your knitting from just a tube into a wearable sock. The heel is my favorite part of the sock and there are so many options to choose from. As you will see in this book we are going a explore a few options for both top down and toe up (see The Fun Part).

Instep

The instep is the top of and widest part of the foot. The shape of the instep can vary from person to person, some being high or some low. When you are knitting a sock with a heel flap and turn, the extra fabric created by the gusset stitches are what accommodates the top of the instep.

Foot

The foot portion of the sock is the "tube" between the heel/instep and the toe. As with the leg, the foot can be worked plain or with colorwork or a textured pattern. Usually the pattern will only be worked on the top (instep) of the foot, with the bottom (sole) stitches worked plain to make the sock comfortable for walking and wearing in shoes.

Toe

The toe is the part of your sock that covers your toes. The toe is formed with either decreases (for a top down sock) or increases (for a toe up sock). The toe shape can vary depending on the desired look or for a certain fit (see On Your Toes).

WHAT IS A VANILLA SOCK?

"Vanilla sock" is a knitter's term that refers to the most basic type of knitted socks worked simply in plain stockinette (stocking stitch). They may be knit toe up or top down with a heel flap and gusset or a simple short row heel, and with a standard wedge toe. The techniques used, like the cast on, bind (cast) off, increases and decreases, are all within the range of skills for a beginner. Vanilla socks do not even necessarily require a specific pattern — you can just work from one end of the sock to the other using basic instructions for each part.

CHAPTER TWO

Methods

"Properly practiced, knitting soothes the troubled spirit, and it doesn't hurt the untroubled spirit either"

ELIZABETH ZIMMERMANN

How Do I Knit Socks?

There is no right or wrong way to knit socks, and I will go so far as to say it is a very personal choice. In the first book I bought about sock knitting, the author used two circular needles. So, I started with that method for distributing my stitches. It made sense to my brain to divide the sock stitches into two parts instead of three or four as for working with DPNs (double-pointed needles). Then a few years later a new book presented the magic loop technique, which made no sense to me at the time, but others had found the answer to their prayers.

My point again, there is no right or wrong way. I say try them all to see what works best for your hands, what makes sense when reading a pattern, and which technique makes the sock knitting process most enjoyable for you.

HOW DO I MANAGE STITCHES ON THE NEEDLES?

Two Circular Needles

With this method you are using two 24in/60cm circular needles and the stitches of the sock are divided into two equal halves. There is a front needle (which usually has the instep stitches) and back needle (which usually has the sole or bottom stitches). The entire sock can be knit without any need to rearrange the stitches and any size sock can be knit. You are also able to try the sock on if needed.

Magic Loop

This method uses one 40–48in/100–120cm long circular needle. As for using two circular needles, the stitches are divided in two equal halves, but the needle points are at one end, and the loop of extra cable of the circular needle is at the other end. There are still front and back needles holding the instep and heel/sole stitches, and there is no need to rearrange the stitches when knitting the sock. The key to this method is making sure the cable of the needle is long enough to provide the needed flexibility. Magic Loop also allows you the opportunity to try the sock on.

DPNs (Double-Pointed Needles)

Working with DPNs is the most traditional and commonly used method of knitting socks. The stitches are distributed onto three or four needles, with one additional needle used for knitting the stitches. This method does make it almost impossible to try the sock on unless the stitches are transferred to scrap yarn.

When knitting the patterns in this book using DPNs, I suggest dividing the stitches by keeping the instep stitches on two needles and the heel stitches on one needle. If a pattern says to work stitches on the front needle, this refers to the needle or needles holding the instep stitches. The back needle refers to the needle or needles holding the heel/sole stitches of the socks.

If you divide your stitches differently, I would recommend using stitch markers to indicate for yourself which are the instep stitches and which are the heel/sole stitches.

One Short Circular Needle

Short circular needles have been used for many years and this method enables the knitter to have all the stitches on one needle. These are usually 9in/23cm long and have a smaller needle shaft. Using a short circular eliminates the "intersections" between multiple needles (see Tips & Tricks: Avoiding Ladders) and allows for a smooth flow of the stitches. All parts of the sock can be knit on the one needle, except the toe. There are fewer stitches at the tip of the toe, with stitches either decreased for top down socks or increased for toe up socks, and the toe circumference is too small to comfortably fit on the circular needle, thus the stitches need to managed using one of the other methods.

WHICH STITCHES ARE ON WHICH NEEDLES?

In some sock patterns there can be design elements, such as colorwork or texture, that require specific placement of the stitches. Some stitches are designated as the top or instep of the sock and are worked in one type of stitch pattern. The remaining stitches are then the sole or bottom stitches and worked in a different stitch pattern.

In these type of patterns there is a need for the distinction between stitches on the needles. When using a method where the stitches are divided in half over two needles, the instep stitches would be on Needle 1 (or, the front needle). The heel and sole stitches are then on Needle 2 (or, the back needle).

When knitting a vanilla sock, designating which stitches belong to which part of the sock is not as critical. For example, when I'm knitting a sock in self-striping yarn and want to insert a contrasting color heel, if the striping yarn's color change happens in the middle of a front or back needle I will undo my stitches back to the beginning of that needle, then introduce the new color for the heel. The goal is to preserve the striping pattern, and which needle you end or begin on is less important.

As my mentor told me many years ago, there are no knitting police, and you can knit the way you want to produce the result you want.

WHAT ABOUT ALTERATIONS AND MODIFICATIONS?

Throughout this book you will find information on customizing cuff styles, sock heels, and various toe options. I have designed this book to allow you, the sock knitter, to customize as you go. A cut and paste sock knitting book if you will!

With this book, other books and patterns in general, there is nothing you can't change to suit your needs or desire.

Cuffs and sock legs can be made longer or shorter, you can change color, the stitch pattern can be swapped for another design.

Heels can be interchanged for other heels. If a heel flap and turn doesn't work for your feet, change to a short row heel instead. Or vice versa.

Some of the patterns in this book are new and some are revisits to my favorite designs. They are here for you to enjoy, learn, and most importantly experiment with.

All of the parts of these patterns can be interchanged. What does that mean? You can take the heel from one pattern and swap it for the heel of another. Don't like a rounded toe, then change it to a wedge toe. Do you love the garter stitch cuff on the EZ Ankle Socks and want to add it to the Rising Up Socks? Go for it!

Should I Knit Toe Up Or Top Down?

There is no correct answer to the question of whether you begin your sock at the toe or the cuff. As explained before (see About This Book), sock knitters seem to naturally divide into Team Toe Up and Team Top Down. I encourage you to try out both ways, and there's no reason you can't be part of both teams!

This decision for each sock, however, must be made before you begin.

Put simply, knitting socks top down is better for fit adjustments, while toe up is better for yarn efficiency and precise foot length control. So here's the breakdown:

Also, remember that sock patterns can be converted. So you are not "locked" in the direction a pattern was originally written. Think of it as another opportunity to be fearless!

Pros for Knitting Socks Top Down

Easy fit checks: you can try on the socks as you knit to ensure the leg and foot length are correct.

Good for beginners: it is a bit easier (and this is relative of course) to learn with a straightforward cast on and overall construction. It is also clearer to see where to start certain areas of the sock, for example the heel.

Variety of heel constructions: you can experiment with different heel flap and turn options that may be easier to knit top down. In my experience there are more heel options written for top down than toe up.

Cons for Knitting Socks Top Down

Potential for wasted yarn: if you miscalculate the length of the leg or foot, you might run out of yarn before reaching the toe.

Less customization: you can't easily adjust the leg length once you've started the foot.

A tight cuff: achieving a comfortable, stretchy cuff can be challenging and is not easily adjustable once you have finished.

Pros for Knitting Socks Toe Up

Maximize yarn usage: you can use every bit of yarn without worrying about running out, or you can carefully use that last precious bit of yarn you've been saving by shortening the leg length if needed.

Customizable foot length: easily adjust the length of the foot to fit your needs.

No grafting: for those of you who dislike grafting stitches, toe up is the way to go.

No picking up stitches: in general, the heel options for toe up do not involve picking up stitches. Of course, there are exceptions to every rule, and some toe up sock designs may incorporate this technique but it tends to be used much less than for top down socks.

Cons for Knitting Socks Toe Up

More technical: requires precise toe shaping with matching increases.

Heel placement: it may be a bit more challenging to place a heel to avoid a foot that is too long or short.

CHAPTER THREE

Planning

"There is nothing impossible
to they who will try"

ALEXANDER THE GREAT

How Do I Prepare?

The two basic things you'll want to have before you put needle to yarn are the pattern you'll be working from and your foot measurements so you know which size to knit. Be sure to check out the Patterns chapter of this book for a fun selection of my sock patterns.

HOW DO I READ PATTERNS?

Reading knitting patterns can seem a bit overwhelming at first, but once you understand all "the parts" it becomes much easier. Here's a basic run-down of how to interpret them. Some of this may seem obvious but it's worth a review and explanation.

Pattern Title and Description

This gives you an overview of the project, including the type of socks and any specific features (e.g., cables, lace, colorwork). The description is important. It gives you most, if not all of the details of the sock. Top down, toe up, texture/design, techniques used, and knitting level. I've heard knitters say they wish they'd known if a pattern was a beginner friendly one or only for advanced knitters.

Yarn and Needles

This lists the type and amount of yarn you need, as well as the recommended needle size. Remember this is the recommended needle size and may not be what you need to use. The needle size listed is what the designer used to get the necessary gauge (tension). It gives the knitter a starting point to help you choose the size needle you will need to achieve the gauge.

Gauge (Tension)

Gauge is the number of stitches and rows per inch or centimeter. It is given for the specific stitch pattern used in the sock — for example stockinette (stocking stitch), ribbing, cables, lace, etc — and helps ensure your finished sock matches the dimensions in the pattern and most importantly, fits your feet.

If you measure and find you are getting more stitches to the inch or centimeter than the pattern says, try using a larger needle. If you are getting too few stitches per inch or centimeter, try using a smaller needle. Remember that the perfect pairing may mean trying different types of needles as well (see Getting Started: Needles).

Sizing

Sock patterns provide measurements and instructions for different sizes.

Understanding what the measurements apply to is very important. In this book I've written each pattern for three sizes — small, medium and large — which relate to the foot circumference. Note that this is different to shoe sizes which are associated with foot length.

Make sure to check the size you want to make (see How Do I Decide Which Size to Knit) and follow the corresponding instructions and numbers. Highlighting all of the instructions and numbers that apply to your size within the pattern can be very helpful and a great way to stay on track.

TAKE IT ONE STEP AT A TIME, AND DON'T BE AFRAID TO LOOK UP UNFAMILIAR TERMS OR TECHNIQUES OR EVEN SUBSTITUTE A TECHNIQUE FOR ONE YOU ARE MORE COMFORTABLE WITH.

Abbreviations and Stitches

Patterns often use abbreviations for stitches (e.g., K for knit, P for purl) and special techniques or instruction names (e.g., K2tog for knit two stitches together, SSK for Slip, Slip, Knit). There's usually a key or legend at the beginning or end of the pattern explaining these. The most important thing to remember is to READ CAREFULLY!

It's not just the abbreviations but the punctuation and symbols that are key.

For example you may come across this instruction in a pattern:

RIGHT SOCK
Round 1: (P2, k2) until end of round.

LEFT SOCK
Round 1: (K2, p2) until end of round.

The parentheses (round brackets) indicate that the knitter is to repeat that pattern to the end of the round.

However, in the instruction below, the knitter only repeats the instruction within the parentheses (round brackets) four times, then follows the rest of the instructions to the end of the round for each needle. At the end of Needle 1, the three sizes are given. Size Small knits 10 stitches, size Medium knits 14 stitches and size Larger knits 18 stitches.

Rounds 1–3:

Needle 1: (P2, k2) 4 times, p2, k10 (14) (18).

Needle 2: Knit all stitches.

Again, this may seem clear to some but I've been asked to clarify directions many a time for many a knitter.

ABBREVIATIONS

BOR	Beginning of round
DPNs	Double-pointed needles
Garter stitch	Knit every row when working back and forth. Alternate knit and purl rounds when working in the round. Two rows/rounds create a garter "ridge"
K	Knit*
KFB	Knit front and back*
Knitwise	Insert needle into stitch as if to knit (this moves a slipped stitch from left to right needle with a twist)
K2tog	Knit 2 stitches together*
M1L/R	Make 1 left/right*
P	Purl*
Purlwise	Insert needle into stitch as if to purl (this moves a slipped stitch from left to right needle without a twist)
P2tog	Purl 2 stitches together*
RS	Right side
RYO	Reverse Yarn Over*
SKL	Slip, Knit, Lift*
Sl	Slip stitch. Pattern will note if the stitch is to be slipped knitwise or purlwise. Unless noted, slip stitches with yarn in back of the work
SSK/SSP	Slip, Slip, Knit/Purl*
St(s)	Stitch(es)
Stockinette (stocking stitch)	Knit all stitches when working in the round. When working back and forth, knit on right side rows and purl on wrong side rows
Tbl	Through the back leg*
Tr st	Triplet stitch †
Tw st	Twin stitch †
WS	Wrong side
WYIF	With yarn held in front of work
YO	Yarn Over*

* See General Techniques for instructions.

† See The Fun Part: Shadow Wrap Short Row Heel for instructions.

How Do I Decide Which Size To Knit?

WHAT IS EASE?

Ease refers to how a knitted item fits. The difference between negative and positive ease in knitting is the size of the finished garment relative to the wearer's body.

Positive ease means the item is larger than the body part it is worn on, as for an oversized sweater (jumper). Negative ease means the item is tighter than the body part it is worn on, which sounds like it would be uncomfortable but remember that knit fabric stretches.

In sock knitting the goal is to have negative ease. In other words, you want the sock to be smaller than the circumference of your foot so the fabric stretches to fit and stays in place, which reduces friction in your shoe.

The general rule is 1in/2.5cm of negative ease, so you want your finished sock circumference to measure that much smaller than your foot circumference.

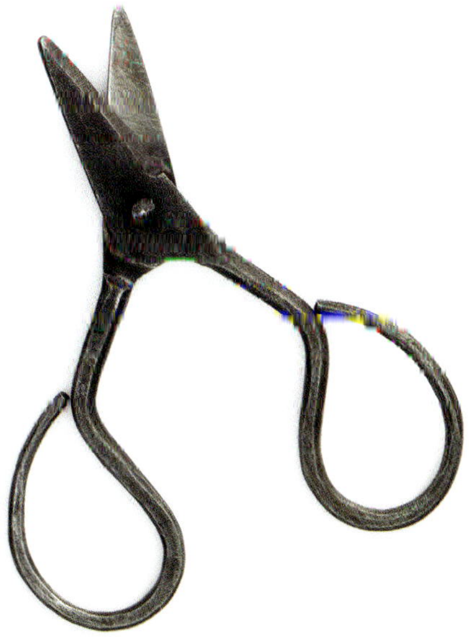

MEASURING YOUR FEET

The main measurement you need to take is your foot circumference, which is measured around the ball (the widest part of your foot, just under your toes).

The foot circumference is generally used when determining size for knitted socks, because you can alter length of the different parts of your sock as indicated in the pattern.

You'll want to use a flexible tape measure to get your foot measurement. Once you have this, select the pattern size that is approximately 1in/2.5cm less than your measurement to account for negative ease as explained previously (see What is Ease). My patterns are written for three sizes, with size Small as 7in/17cm, size Medium as 8in/20cm and size Large as 9in/23cm. These sizes determine how many stitches are cast on for the pattern.

For example, for a 9in/23cm foot circumference, subtract 1in/2.5cm for negative ease, so an 8in/20cm finished circumference, multiplied by a gauge of 8 stitches per 1in/2.5cm works out to 64 stitches for the "average" medium sized foot.

Creating a Template

If you want to customize your socks to your own feet for a really good fit, it does require some math and a bit of work on your part. So let's work together for what we want — great fitting, comfy socks.

We are going to make a template of your foot. This template will have all the information you need about your foot. The most important thing is taking good and accurate measurements. Yes, you can use foot rulers once your sock is in progress, but a personalized template will give you the information you need to make custom fit socks.

The best medium for this is a piece of light/soft cardboard, like a breakfast cereal box.

1. Cut one side of the box, stand on it with one foot on the cardboard the other foot lined up next to it. Now trace the outline of your feet. You may need to ask someone for help here. If not be careful you don't fall over (ask me how I know).

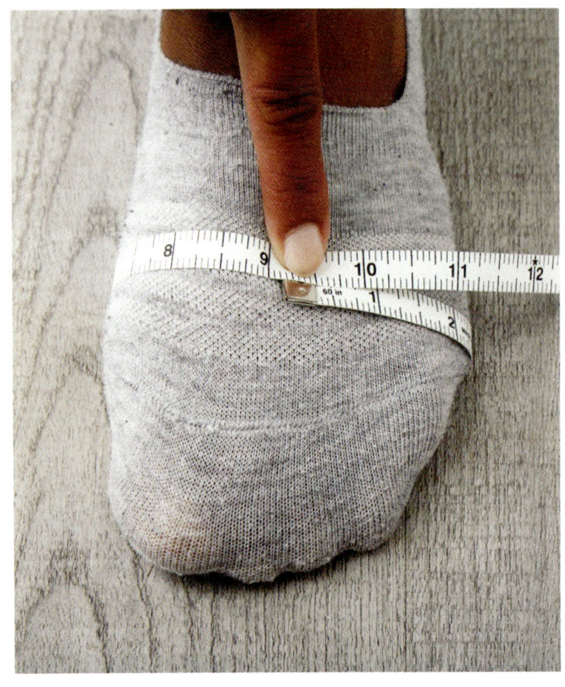

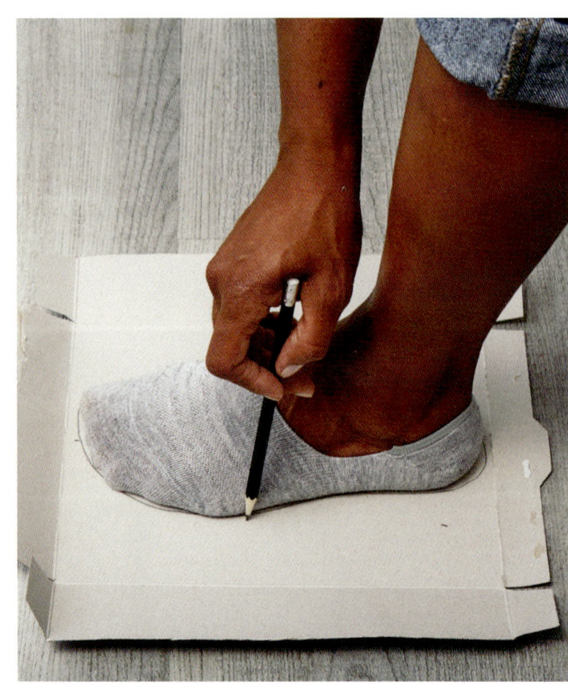

2. You are now going to mark the following things on the template:

- Length from big toe to heel, for example 9¼in/23.5cm.
- The width of the ball of your foot, for example 3½in/9cm.
- The location of the base of your big toe (toe decrease line for Team Top Down).
- The distance between the base of your big toe and the start of the slope of your arch (leg line).
- The location of your ankle bone. To add this, hold the pencil/pen in line with your ankle bone and mark that point on the template. Then draw a line across the template (heel line for Team Toe Up).

These all represent the measurements of your foot, and you now have a physical guide to knit your socks.

Using the Template

Whether you are knitting top down or toe up you can insert the template into your sock in progress to know where to start a toe or heel.

For top down socks, the toe decreases start at the base of the big toe.

For toe up socks, the heel starts at the heel line, which aligns with your ankle bone.

As you can see, this is a simple yet invaluable tool.

I SUGGEST LAMINATING THE TEMPLATE TO PRESERVE IT AND TO FACILITATE EASE OF USE.

CHAPTER FOUR

Let's Knit!

"You can't use up creativity, the more you use, the more you have"

MAYA ANGELOU

How Do I Begin?

You've got your perfect pairing of yarn and needles (see Getting Started), you've decided whether you are Team Toe Up and Team Top Down (see Methods) and you've picked your pattern (see Patterns). All of these determine which cast on you can choose from. Here are a few of my favorites, but you can always choose your own preferred technique instead.

TOP DOWN CAST ONS

Long Tail Cast On

1. Leaving a very long tail, start with a slip knot on the needle and hold it in your right hand. The yarn tail after the slip knot should be approximately 20–28in/50–70cm long before the loop from the tail end, depending on your size. Note that this is a very generous approximation of length because you don't want to run out of yarn before completing the cast on.

2. Put your first finger and thumb (left hand) between the strand, hold the two strands with the rest of your hand and bring your fingers down into a "slingshot" position (A).

3. Insert the needle into the loop around the thumb from below (B).

4. Insert the needle into the loop around your first finger from above and behind (C).

5. Catch the yarn and pull it through the loop around your thumb (D).

6. Remove your thumb from the "slingshot" (E), then tighten up the stitch by replacing your thumb and getting back into position to make the next stitch (F).

Repeat Steps 2–6 until you have cast on the desired number of stitches.

Then continue to work the cuff of your sock.

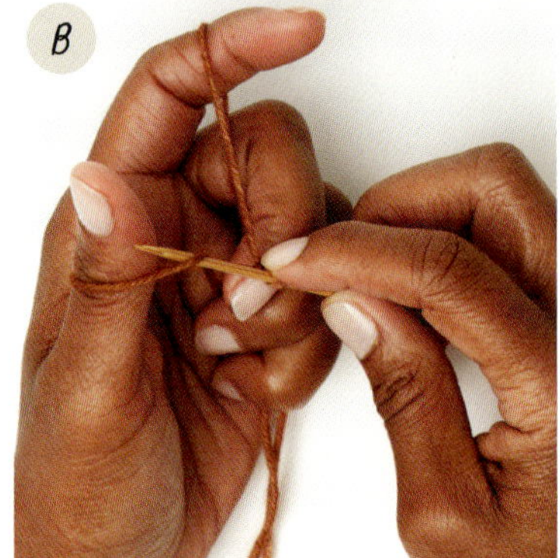

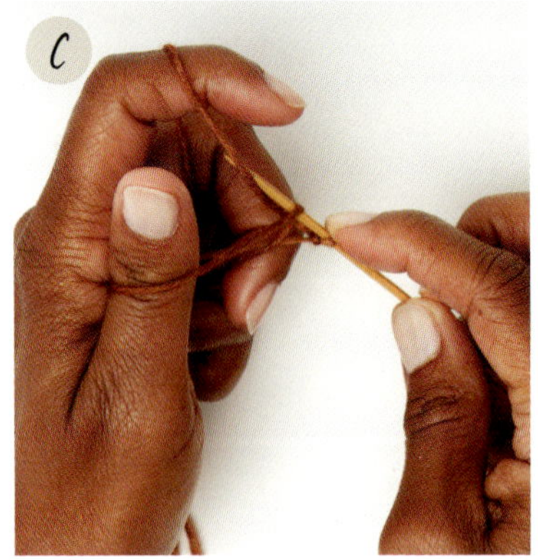

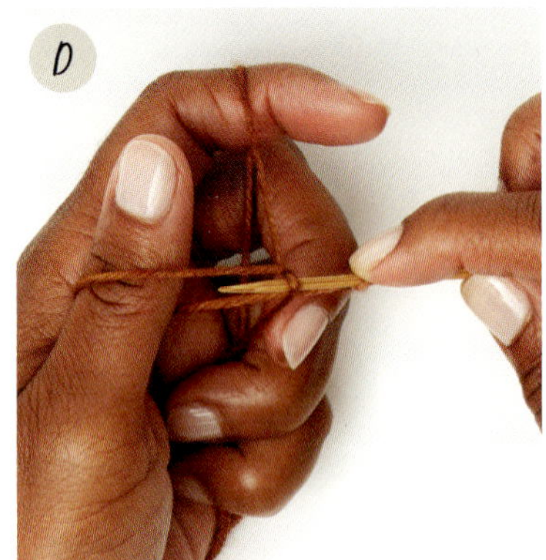

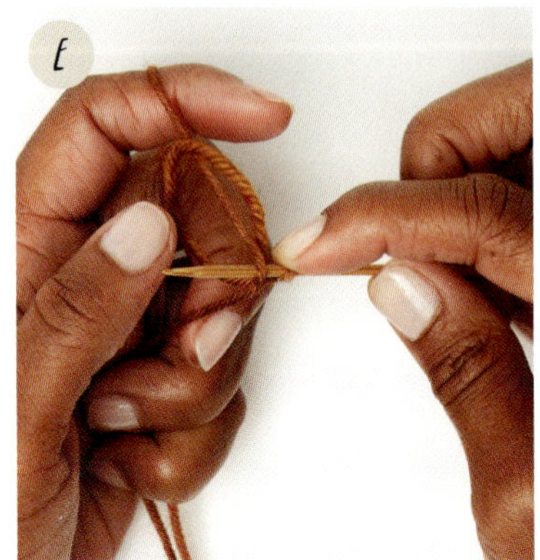

German Twisted Cast On

The German Twisted Cast On, also known as Old Norwegian Cast On, is a variation of the Long Tail Cast On but has a more defined, sturdy yet equally flexible edge. I like to pair this cast on with a Garter Stitch or 1x1 Rib cuff.

1. Start with a backward loop around the needle, leaving a yarn tail approximately 3 times longer than you would for a long tail cast on. (This cast on "eats" a bit more yarn than usual.)

2. Put your first finger and thumb (left hand) between the strand, hold the two strands with the rest of your hand and bring your fingers down into a "slingshot" position (A).

3. Go around the loop that's around your thumb coming from below (B).

4. Insert the needle into that thumb loop coming from above (C).

5. Bring the needle out on the left side (D) (the side facing toward you).

6. Swing the needle up and over to catch the working yarn/strand on your index finger coming from behind (E).

7. Untwist the loop around your thumb and pull the yarn through the untwisted loop (F).

8. Remove your thumb from the loop (G) and reposition it back into the slingshot position, while tightening up the newly made stitch slightly on the needle (H). This will also set up creating the next stitch.

Repeat Steps 3–8 until you cast on the desired number of stitches.

Then continue to work the cuff of your sock.

A

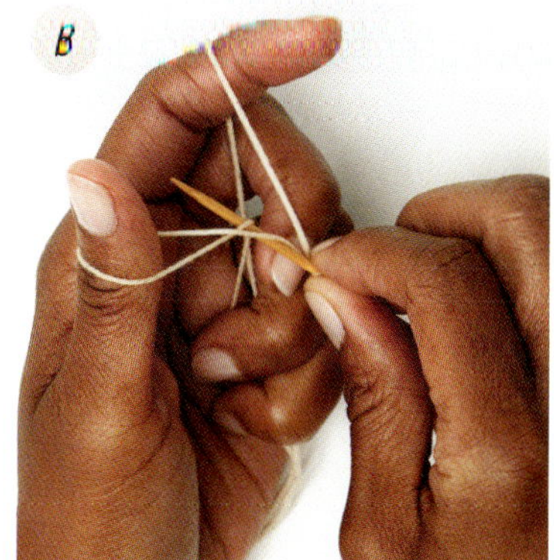

B

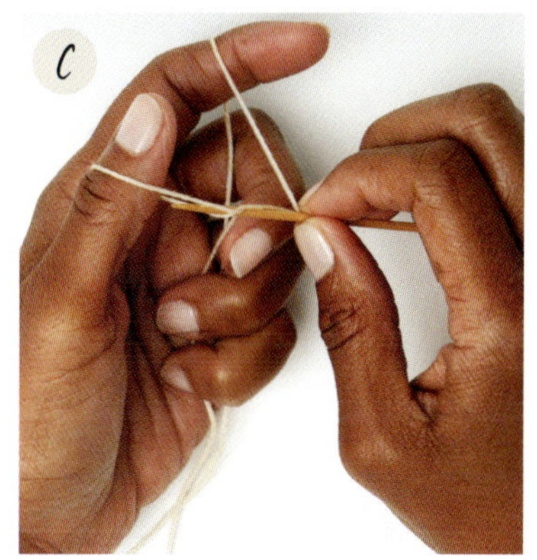

C

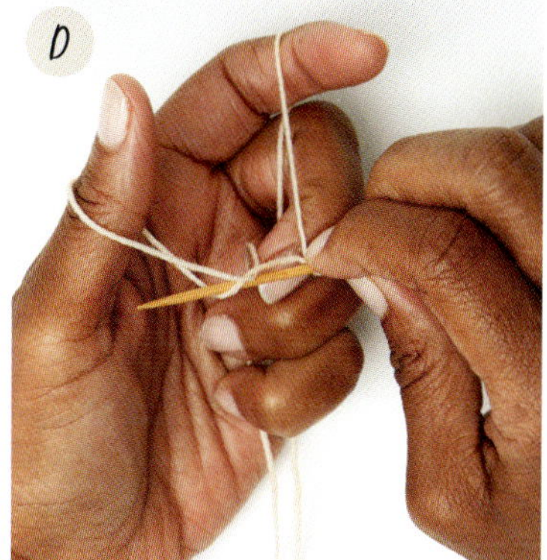

D

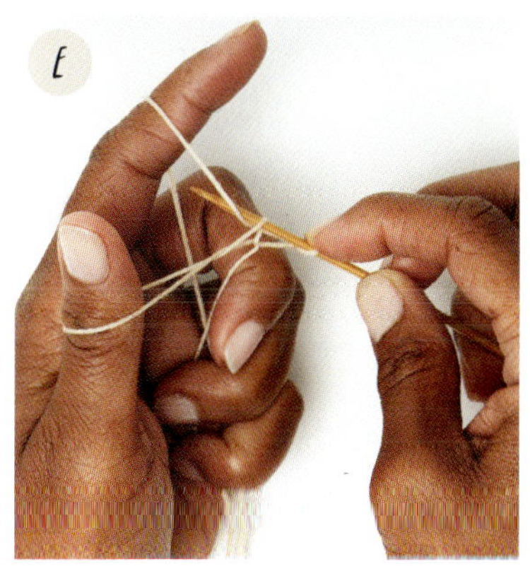

E

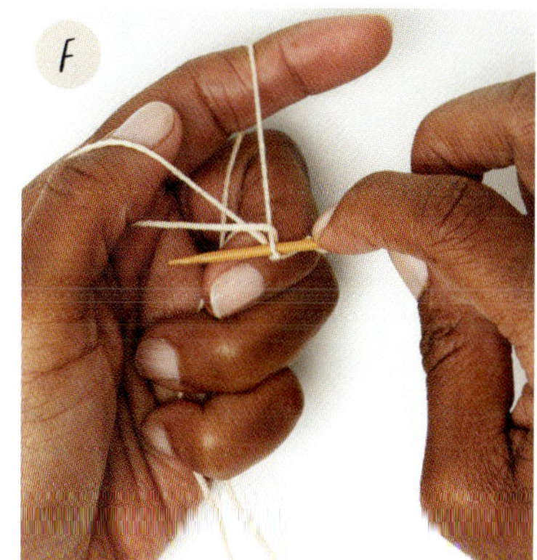

F

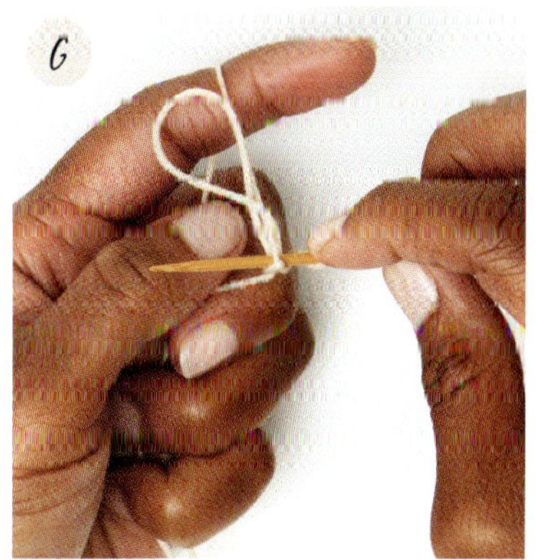

G

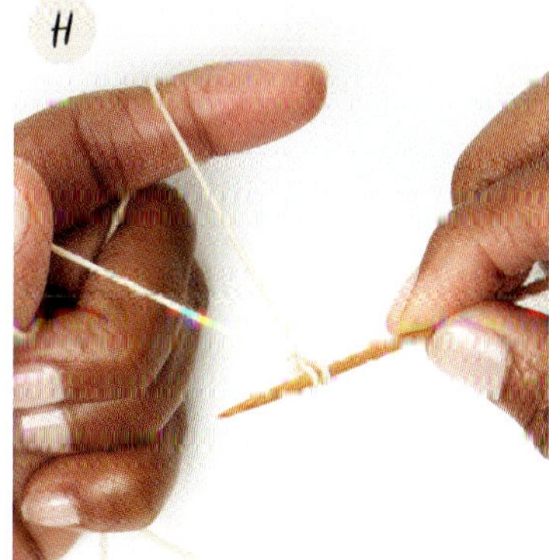

H

TOE UP CAST ONS

Turkish Cast On

The Turkish Cast On creates a great start for toe up socks. It is also very beginner friendly (always a plus).

This cast on is worked over two circular needles or two circular needle points.

1. Start with a backward loop on one needle. You can leave a shorter tail for this one but still long enough to comfortably weave in later.

2. Hold your needles parallel, with the backward loop on the top needle and the tips pointing to the left (A).

3. Wrap the working yarn around both needles, away from you counter-clockwise (anti-clockwise) (B).

4. Continue wrapping the yarn around both needles (C). Each wrap creates 2 stitches (one on each needle). So, if you need to cast on 20 stitches, wrap the yarn 10 times. Do not count the backward loop as a stitch.

5. Once you have enough wraps/stitches, rotate your needles clockwise so the tips point to the right (D).

6. Slide out the bottom needle (E). The lower portion of stitches will be held on the cable of the circular needle.

7. Now, knit into the first loop on the remaining (top) needle (F), then continue knitting across all the stitches on this needle.

8. Rotate your work, rearrange your circular needle(s) so the unworked stitches are on the needle tip, and the previously worked stitches are held on the cable of the circular needle (G). Carefully drop the backward loop, then knit across these stitches (H).

Then continue to work the toe of your sock.

A

B

C

D

E

F

G

H

Judy's Magic Cast On

This cast on is my absolute favorite for toe up socks. There are a few different ways to work this cast on but this method will get the stitches properly lined up on the needles, with no need to reposition them.

This cast on is worked over two circular needles, two circular needle points or two DPNs (double-pointed needles).

1. Leaving a long tail end of yarn (the length depends on how many stitches you are casting on), make a backward loop and place it onto one of the needles. Then hold both needles in your right hand with tips pointing to the left, with the needle with the backward loop as the top needle (A). The yarn ends are held behind the needles.

2. Hold the yarn ends in the palm of your left hand, insert your first finger and thumb between the strands (like a slingshot). Keep the tail end of yarn over your first finger and the working yarn (the yarn from the ball) over your thumb.

3. Using your right hand to create a seesaw motion, bring the bottom needle over the yarn on your first finger (B), bring the yarn down and between the two needles, creating the first loop (C).

4. Next, bring the top needle down and under the strand on your thumb between the two needles (D) creating a loop on the top needle (E).

5. Repeat Steps 3 & 4 alternately, adding one stitch at a time to the top and bottom needles (F) until you have the desired number of stitches.

6. Once you have the correct number of stitches, rotate the needles so that they are pointing to the right and in the correct position to start knitting. Pull out the bottom needle to begin the round (G) or if using DPNs use another needle to begin the round.

7. You will notice that there is a row of purl bumps on one side. These indicate the wrong side of your knitting, or rather the soon-to-be inside of your toe.

8. The top needle is Needle 1 and the bottom needle is Needle 2. The working yarn should be coming from Needle 2 (H).

Then continue to work the toe of your sock.

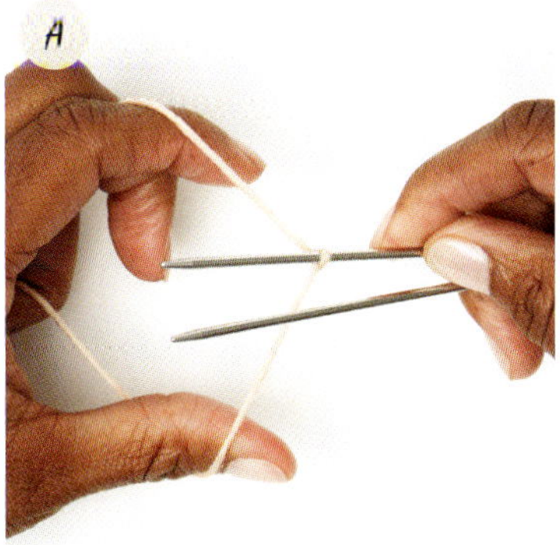

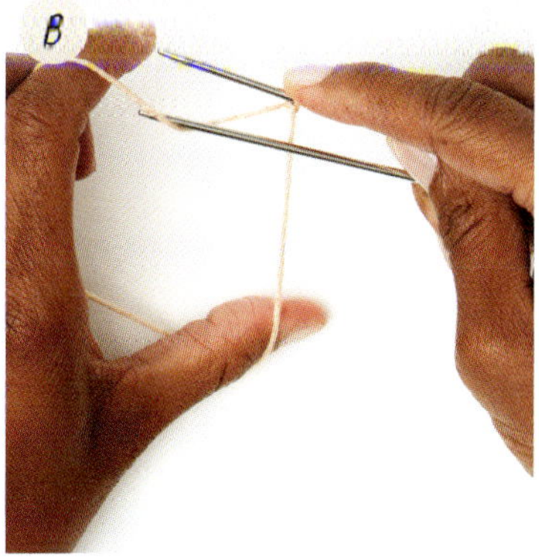

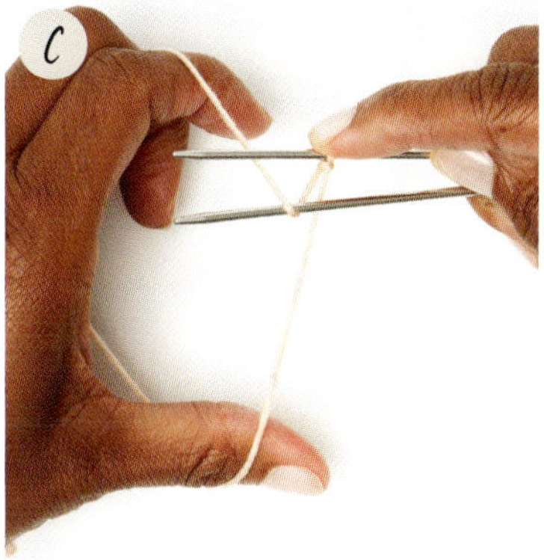

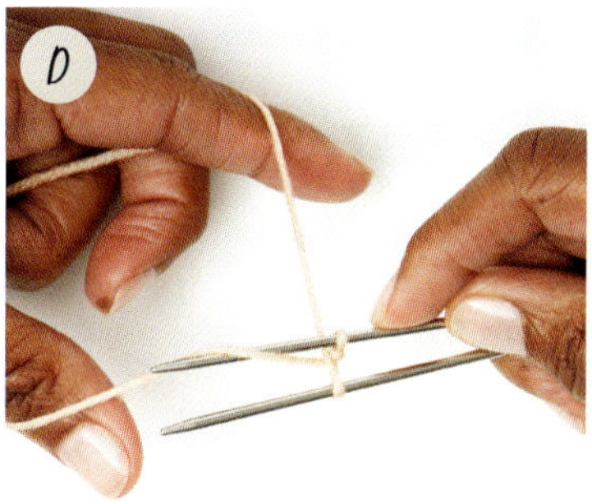

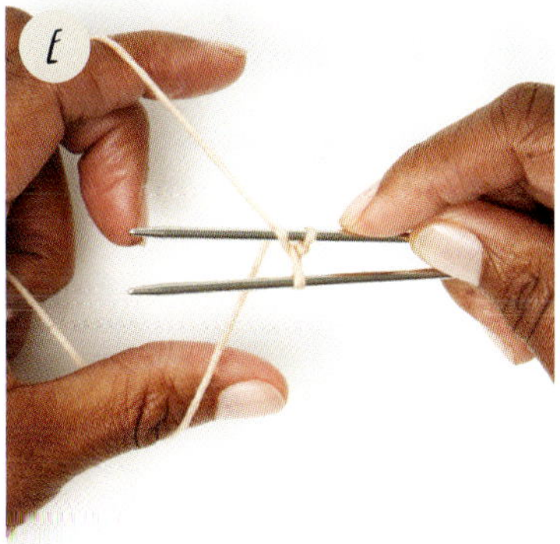

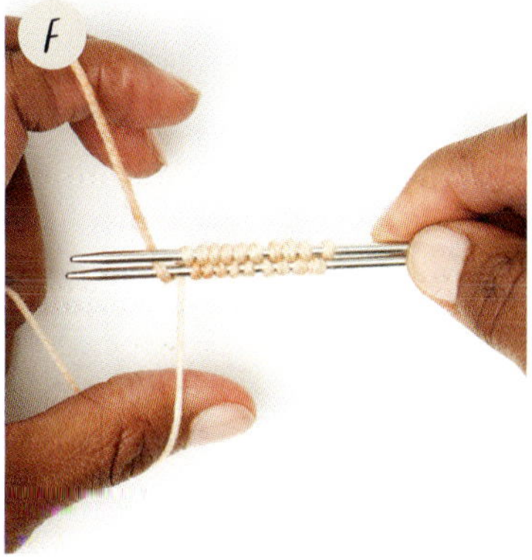

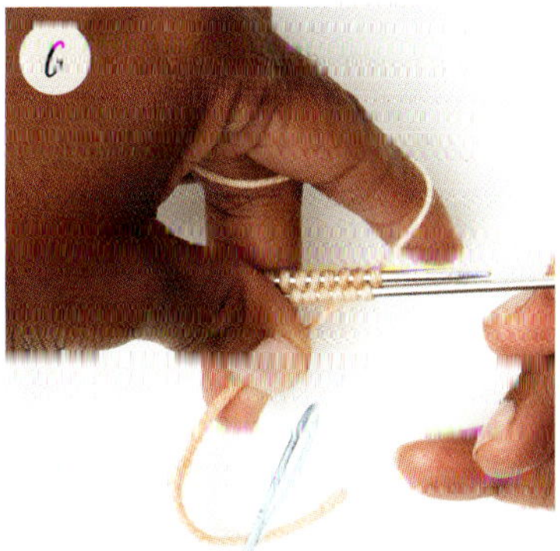

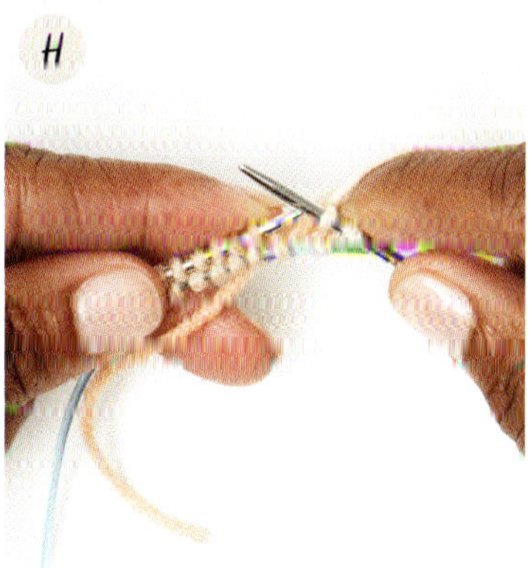

CHAPTER FIVE

Knitting Along

"Nothing is impossible. The word itself says 'I'm possible'!"

AUDREY HEPBURN

Where To Next?

I've heard many new sock knitters say, knitting socks seems hard, I'm scared, I don't like tiny needles but guess what — you've made it this far, and I'm so proud of you!!

Team Top Down will be working on the cuff next (see What Are My Cuff Options), then the straight run of the leg. Team Toe Up will need to pop forward to the On Your Toes chapter before coming back to work on the length of the foot.

These "straight" parts of the sock can all be customized for your preference and your size, knitting to the length that works for you.

Then both teams will be ready for The Fun Part in the following chapter.

WHAT DOES KNIT TO DESIRED LENGTH MEAN?

The instruction "knit to desired length" in a pattern means that you should continue knitting in the pattern or stitch specified until the sock reaches the length you want or need before you start the heel or toe, or before working the cuff.

Check Pattern Measurements

Does the pattern tell you to knit until the sock measures 2in/5cm less than desired length on the foot? For a top down sock, the 2in/5cm measurement refers to the depth of the toe section. However, not everyone has toes that are the same length, so you may need to knit the foot a bit longer or shorter.

The same applies for the heel when working toe up. The instructions say to knit to 2in/5cm less than the total length of the foot before you start the heel. The pattern may say that the foot length is 7½in/19cm for a medium size but that may not apply to you. Knit to 2in/5cm less than the length of your own foot (see Planning: How Do I Decide Which Size to Knit).

Use a Measuring Tool

As you knit, use a ruler or measuring tape to check the length of your work periodically. This helps ensure you stop at the correct length. Depending on the knitting method you've chosen you may also be able to try on the sock. That is my go-to method.

If you created a sock template (see Planning: How Do I Decide Which Size to Knit) that will contain all the needed information to make your custom sock, and let you know when to start the heel/toe depending on if you are Team Toe Up or Team Top Down.

So, "knit to desired length" gives you the flexibility to customize the length of your sock based on your personal preference or fit requirements.

KNITTING THE LEG

The leg of the sock is a one of the sweet spots (the other is the foot). Whether you are knitting in simple stockinette (stocking stitch), colorwork, or texture, this is the place in the sock where you "hit your stride". You are sock knitting and enjoying every stitch. There is a rhythm to these long stretches of one easy stitch after another.

KNITTING THE FOOT

The tube of the foot is another easy knitting section, though some socks may have the sole and instep stitches worked in different stitch patterns (for example, plain on the sole and colorwork on the instep), but for the patterns in this book I've kept it simple and all foot sections are worked plain.

You'll also need to know when to stop knitting the foot. And this is where your foot template (see Planning: How Do I Decide Which Size to Knit) is most useful.

Where to Start the Toe (for Team Top Down)

When working top down, continue the foot until you need to begin the toe decreases. Now some people may use very detailed math equations to decide where the toe shaping begins but I will keep it simple for you. If you have knit socks before then you may have your own preference of how long the foot measures or how many rounds to knit before the toe shaping. However, if you are new to sock knitting, then this is how I do it.

Place your foot template into the sock in progress, making sure to lay it on a flat surface. If your knitting reaches the toe line then you are ready to start the toe decreases. If not, measure the distance between your knitting and the toe line on the template, and also check your gauge (tension) (see Planning: How Do I Read Patterns) to determine how many rounds to knit.

For example, if your gauge comes to 10 rounds per 1in/2.5cm and you measured ½in/1.25cm before the toe line, then you have 5 rounds to knit before you start the toe shaping. When calculating, don't worry about fractions or extra digits: simply round down to the nearest whole number. It's always better for your sock to need to stretch a bit then be too big.

Where to Start the Heel (for Team Toe Up)

When working toe up, you'll use the same way to decide where to start the heel.

Place your foot template into the sock in progress. If the knitting reaches the heel line then you are ready to start the heel shaping. Otherwise, measure the distance between your knitting and the heel line on the template and check your gauge (tension) to calculate how many rounds to knit.

For example, if your gauge comes to 9 rounds per 1in/2.5cm and you measured ½in/1.25cm before the heel line, then you have 4.5 rounds to knit before you start the heel. But of course you can't knit a half a round so as explained previously, round down to 4 rounds.

What Are My Cuff Options?

No matter the direction of your sock knitting most cuff options can be applied to both top down and toe up. This section could be a book all by itself but I will keep things simple and share the more commonly used cuff options.

I tend to use the versatile 2x2 Rib cuff but choosing an alternative can be fun and really take your sock knitting skills up a notch or two.

2x2 Rib

This cuff is usually knit over an even number of stitches that is divisible by 4. Start by knitting 2 stitches and purling 2 stitches, and repeat (k2, p2) to the end of the round.

1x1 Rib

This cuff is knit over any even number of stitches. You can start with a knit or a purl stitch, then just alternate between the two to the end of the round.

Twisted Rib

If you knit into the back leg of a stitch instead of the front leg this causes the stitch to twist. You can change either 2x2 Rib or 1x1 Rib into the twisted version. This produces a very elegant cuff design, but note that it is a bit less elastic then using untwisted stitches.

Garter Stitch

I love garter stitch so much and while it is not a common cuff choice, it can be very cozy on a shorty sock (see Patterns: EZ Ankle Socks). The trick is working the cuff with a needle one size smaller than the needle used for the rest of the sock. It makes the cuff more snug since there is less horizontal stretch to the fabric produced.

Cuffs and Needle Size

Many patterns suggest using a needle one size smaller for the cuff than the one used for the rest of the sock. Truth be told I am of two minds about whether this is necessary. I recommend it when working the main pattern in colorwork and for ankle socks specifically, but for a regular vanilla sock, it may not be needed. This is why experimenting and practicing are so important.

CHAPTER SIX

The Fun Part

"You don't knit because you are patient. You are patient because you knit"

STEPHANIE PEARL-MCPHEE

Is Knitting A Heel Scary?

Absolutely no, the heel is not scary at all, it's the fun part!

There are many kinds of sock heels out there to experiment with and all of them are beautiful and very interesting to knit. However, for the beginner too many options can feel very overwhelming and daunting. In many cases the sock knitter is left not quite knowing where to start and which heel is best for them.

In this chapter I explain the heel flap method for top down socks, the heel flap method for toe up socks, and a short row heel that can be worked for all socks. Both heel flap and short row heel types are customizable for the best fit for your sock.

TOP DOWN HEEL FLAP AND TURN

This heel is commonly used for top down socks. The heel flap and turn is knit over half the stitches in your sock to create an L shaped portion needed to hold your heel.

Heel Flap

The heel flap is a square or rectangular piece of fabric that's worked flat to cover the back of your heel. It is knit over half the total number of sock stitches, back and forth in rows.

The heel flap can be knit plain, with slip stitches, textured (garter stitch) or even in colorwork. You can customize the flap longer or shorter as needed.

Stitches are slipped at the start of the heel flap rows so they can be picked up later for the gusset. You can slip the stitches purlwise (moving them from left needle to right needle without twisting), but I prefer to slip the first stitch of each row knitwise (inserting the needle as if to knit). The twist adds extra strength when picking up the gusset stitches.

Heel Turn

The heel turn is a short row technique used to create a pocket where your heel fits. It is worked across the stitches from the heel flap. "Short rows" means that you don't knit all the stitches on the needle before turning to work the other side. This leaves a gap in the fabric. The turn works to decrease the stitches on either side of the gap to "bridge it" and to shape the heel.

The heel turn can be round, 'V' shaped or square (see Patterns: Alacrity Socks). The shaping affects the fit and look of the heel. One style is not better than another, it comes down to personal preference, so experiment with different patterns and heel turns to find what works best for your own feet.

Picking Up Stitches

Knit across half the heel stitches and place a marker to indicate the center bottom of the foot and the beginning of the round. Knit the rest of heel stitches. Pick up and knit 1 stitch in each slipped stitch along the edge of the heel flap (A) plus 1 stitch in the intersection between the end of the heel flap and the instep stitches (B). Place a marker to indicate the right side of the foot.

Work across the top of the foot (the instep stitches) in pattern. Place a marker to indicate the left side of the foot. Pick up and knit 1 stitch in the intersection between the instep stitches and the beginning of the heel flap and 1 stitch in each slipped stitch along the second edge the heel flap (C).

Knit across the first half of the heel stitches until you reach the beginning of the round marker.

You are back to working in the round and ready to start the gusset.

Working the Gusset

Round 1 (decrease round): Knit to 3 stitches before the marker indicating the right side of the foot, k2tog, k1, slip the right side marker, continue in pattern across the instep stitches, slip the left side marker, k1, ssk, knit to the beginning of round marker. 2 stitches have been decreased.

Round 2 (even round): Knit to right side marker, slip marker, work the instep stitches in pattern, slip left side marker, knit to the beginning of round marker.

Repeat Rounds 1 & 2 until all of the heel flap stitches have been decreased and you've returned to your original number of stitches for your size. Continue knitting on the foot.

KNIT THROUGH THE BACK LEG ON THE HEEL FLAP STITCHES ONLY ON THE FIRST ROUND OF THE GUSSET, INCLUDING THE INTERSECTION STITCHES. THIS HELPS TIGHTEN THE BASE OF THOSE STITCHES AND ELIMINATES POTENTIAL HOLES.

How to Customize the Heel Flap and Turn

It took me a long time to appreciate the brilliance of a heel flap and turn and it has become one of my favorites. Why did it take me so long? To be honest I wasn't knitting the heel flap long enough and so the heel "rode down" into my shoes. I thought I had to follow the rule that the flap should be as long as it is wide. For example, if you have 32 heel stitches the flap should be 32 rows long, which would produce 16 slip stitches along the side of the flap. I'm here to tell you that is not true. You are in charge of your sock and you can customize anything for a better fit.

If you are substituting the Heel Flap and Turn in another pattern, or if you have changed the number of cast-on stitches to adjust for your size, then the following formula will tell you how to customize the number of stitches needed for the Heel Flap and Turn.

To find the number of stitches for the heel flap, simply divide the total number stitches for your sock by 2. For example, 68 stitches divided by 2 equals 34. Your heel flap will be 34 stitches wide. Slipping the first stitch of every row, work in rows until the flap is the length required. This may be 34 rows to match your stitches, or as I've found for myself, I knit the heel flap longer to accommodate my higher instep.

Please remember to make a note of how many slip stitches you have created on the heel flap because that is how many stitches you will be picking up for the gusset. Later when you start the gusset decreases, continue until you are back to your original number of stitches.

Now to calculate the heel turn, divide the number of heel flap stitches by 2, then add an additional 2 stitches. For example, 34 heel flap stitches divided by 2 equals 17 which is the number of stitches in the heel turn. Now add 2, which equals 19. The first decrease of the heel turn begins after you have worked 2 stitches past the center of the heel. Remember this includes the slipped stitch.

In pattern form that will look like this:

Row 1 (RS): Sl 1, k18, ssk, k1, turn work.

Row 2 (WS): Sl 1, p5, p2tog, p1, turn work.

Row 3 (RS): Sl 1, knit to 1 st before the gap created by the previous row, ssk with 1 st from each side of the gap (this closes the gap), k1, turn work.

Row 4 (WS): Sl 1, purl to 1 st before the gap created in the previous row, p2tog with 1 st from each side of the gap, p1, turn work.

Rep Rows 3 & 4 until all the side stitches have been worked on the heel.

SHADOW WRAP SHORT ROW HEEL

While there are many short row heels, such as Wrap and Turn, German Short Row, Japanese Short Row, my favorite as some of you may know is the Shadow Wrap Short Row Heel. You can generally interchange one short row heel for another in a pattern. Even better, this heel is worked the same for either Team Top Down or Team Toe Up!

The Shadow Wrap Short Row heel is very simple and quick to understand. It is customizable and has perfectly symmetrical increases and decreases. The shadow wraps are worked as Twin Stitches and Triplet Stitches.

Twin and Triplet Stitches are very similar. The primary difference is that a Twin Stitch is formed by working into a regular stitch and a Triplet Stitch is formed by working into a Twin Stitch. In other words, a Triplet Stitch is only created from a Twin Stitch.

Twin Stitch (Tw st)

Twin Stitch (RS, knit side): Knit to the indicated stitch. With the right needle lift the right leg of the stitch below the next stitch on the left needle (A) and place the lifted strand onto the left needle. Knit into the lifted strand (B) and slip the new stitch back to the left needle. There are now two stitches coming out of the one stitch (C).

Twin Stitch (WS, purl side): Purl to the indicated stitch. Slip the next stitch to the right needle, then with the left needle lift the leg of the stitch below the slipped stitch (D). Purl into the lifted strand (E) and return both of the purled stitches to the left needle (F). There are now two stitches coming out of the same stitch.

Resolve a twin stitch by knitting (on the right side of the work) or purling (on the wrong side of the work) all the strands of the stitch together as a single stitch when you come across a twin stitch on the subsequent row or round.

Triplet Stitch (Trpt)

Triplet Stitch (RS, knit side): Knit to the indicated twin stitch. Lift the right leg of the stitch below the twin stitches with the right needle (A) and place the lifted strand onto the left needle. Knit into the lifted strand (B) then slip the stitch back to the left needle. There are now three stitches coming out of the same stitch (C).

Triplet Stitch (WS, purl side): Purl to the indicated twin stitch. Slip both strands of the twin stitch onto the right needle. With the left needle lift the left leg of the stitch below the twin stitch (D) and purl into the lifted stitch, then return all three strands to the left needle (E). There are now three stitches coming out of the same lower stitch (F).

Resolve a triplet stitch in the same way as for a twin stitch, by knitting or purling all the strands of the stitch together as a single stitch when you come across a triplet stitch on the subsequent row or round.

Knitting the Shadow Wrap Heel

The Shadow Wrap Short Row Heel is worked by dividing the heel stitches into three sections: the center stitches, left of center stitches and right of center stitches. On the first half of the heel, twin stitches are created row-by-row by working into the side stitches ("decreasing" to the plain center stitches). On the second half of the heel, triple stitches are created row by row working into the twin stitches ("increasing" back to the original number of heel stitches).

Using a Contrast Color for the Heel

If you are working in more than one color (for example see Patterns: Helical Socks), when you are ready to start the heel, the yarn that will be used for the heel must be on the right side of the sock and ready to knit across to form the first twin stitch (A).

The other color can be positioned anywhere on the side with the instep stitches (B).

Customize for Your Yarn

Here is how to customize the Shadow Wrap Short Row Heel using the yarn weight of your choice in the pattern of your choice based on the number of stitches you are knitting for your size.

Most of the time the stitches will divide evenly, though sometimes they will not. Let's look at the math...

EVEN DISTRIBUTION

If, for example, your DK (light worsted) weight medium sized sock has 48 stitches, that is 24 stitches for the instep and 24 stitches for the sole/heel.

24 divided by 3 equals 8.

8 center stitches, 8 left of center stitches, and 8 right of center stitches.

So, you will knit across your heel to the last stitch, knit a twin stitch, turn, purl to the last stitch, purl a twin stitch, turn... and continue until there are 8 plain center stitches, 8 twin stitches on the left, and 8 twin stitches on the right.

Then continue to the second half of the heel stitches as instructed in the pattern.

How Do I Fix Other Heel Issues?

There is no need to panic when things go wrong with your knitting. Staying calm always helps, and going step by step to address and fix the problem is the only way through.

Fixing a Dropped Twin or Triple Stitch

Try as we may to avoid them, dropped stitches do happen. But when they happen in a twin or triple stitch, the panic sets in and the big question is asked, Now What Do I do? Here's what you do. First take a deep breath and look at your work closely.

In order to create the twin and triple stitches, extra loops are added to a main stitch. When those loops fall off they will not fully "drop" but they need to be replaced back into the main stitch. Using a small crochet hook, pull each loop through the main stitch and place it onto the needle (A).

You'll need to do this once for a twin stitch and twice for a triple stitch to restore the dropped stitches that were lost. Once the stitches are back on the needle you can continue knitting.

How to Avoid the Color Blip in Shadow Row Short Heels

How you ever noticed a little "blip" of color in one corner of a shadow wrap short row heel (B)?

Firstly you may wonder why this happens. When knitting a shadow wrap short row heel, on the first row (the knit side) the first twin stitch is created in the stitch from the previous row, which may be the main color if knitting in a contrasting color. That stitch is being stretched due to the effect of adding a second stitch. However on the purl side the first twin stitch is being created in the new color or extra stitch added from the first row, so the stretch is still there but not visible.

It can be more noticeable when you are working with highly contrasting colors. To be honest when it's not that visible, I will often not worry about it! However, if you prefer to avoid it showing, this is what you can do.

Once you have knitted the entire heel and have returned to knitting in the round, work as follows: take a darning needle or even the tip of your knitting needle and gently pull on the right leg of the stretched stitch, then pull the left leg of the stitch next to it. Continue pulling the left leg, then right leg until the excess yarn has been "absorbed" into the adjoining stitches. The blip will disappear and the corners of your heel will be neat and tidy.

CHAPTER SEVEN

On Your Toes

"Once you face your fear, nothing is ever as hard as you think"

OLIVIA NEWTON-JOHN

What Are My Toe Options?

This chapter will provide you with three toe shaping options that can be knit using any sock knitting technique. I suggest trying them all to find the one that best fits your toes. And if you're Team Top Down, your sock is almost done, and I don't know about you but I'm usually doing a little happy dance at this point.

WEDGE TOE

The Wedge Toe is "standard" and most commonly used. The decreases are done every other round creating a trapezoid shape for the toe area.

Pro: The instructions are easy to follow as you alternate between decrease/increase and plain rounds. This is also a good one to start with when learning.

Con: Some people find this shape toe a bit "sharp" at the corners and it bears the least resemblance to the natural shape of one's toes. And in anticipation of the question, no you can't feel the "points" when you wear them, or rather I've never heard anyone comment or complain.

Top Down Wedge Toe Instructions

Round 1 (decrease round):

Needle 1/Front Cable: K1, ssk, knit to 3 sts before the end, k2tog, k1.

Needle 2/Back Cable: K1, ssk, knit to 3 sts before the end, k2tog, k1.

Round 2: Knit all sts.

Repeat Rounds 1 & 2 until 20 sts remain (10 sts on each needle). Cut a tail about 12in/30.5cm long and graft stitches together (see Finish Line: Grafting Made Easy).

Toe Up Wedge Toe Instructions

Note: You can use your preferred increase method for Round 2.

Cast on 20 sts, with 10 sts on each needle.

Round 1: Knit all sts.

Round 2 (increase round):

Needle 1/Front Cable: K1, kfb, knit to 2 sts before the end, skl, k1.

Needle 2/Back Cable: K1, kfb, knit to 2 sts before the end, skl, k1.

Repeat Rounds 1 & 2 until you have 56 (62) (72) sts in total (28 (32) (36) sts on each needle). Rearrange the stitches as you prefer for your needles before beginning the foot.

ROUND TOE

The Round Toe is a bit more anatomically friendly and gives a round shape to the end of the toe. The eliminates the "points" and gives the toes a bit more wiggle room.

Pro: This toe shaping is more customized and better accommodates the natural shape of the toes. There is also less distortion in the toe when wearing the sock.

Con: You have to pay a bit more attention to the instructions since they change about halfway through. This isn't a major problem, not at all, just remember to keep track of your rounds and "read" your knitting carefully.

Top Down Round Toe Instructions

Round 1 (decrease round):

Needle 1/Front Cable: K1, ssk, knit to 3 sts before the end, k2tog, k1.

Needle 2/Back Cable: K1, ssk, knit to 3 sts before the end, k2tog, k1.

Round 2: Knit all sts.

Repeat Rounds 1 & 2 until 40 sts remain (20 sts on each needle). Repeat only Round 1 (decrease round) until 20 sts remain (10 sts on each needle).

Cut a tail about 12in/30.5cm long and graft stitches together (see Finish Line: Grafting Made Easy).

Toe Up Round Toe Instructions

Note: You can use your preferred increase method for Round 2.

Using the cast on method of your choice, cast on 20 sts, with 10 sts on each needle.

Round 1: Knit all sts.

Round 2 (increase round):

Needle 1/Front Cable: K1, kfb, knit to 2 sts before the end, skl, k1.

Needle 2/Back Cable: K1, kfb, knit to 2 sts before the end, skl, k1.

Repeat Rounds 1 & 2 until there are 40 sts in total (20 sts on each needle).

Repeat only Round 2 (increase round) until you have 56 (62) (72) sts in total (28 (32) (36) sts on each needle). Rearrange the stitches as you prefer for your needles before beginning the foot.

ANATOMICAL TOE

The Anatomical Toe most closely resembles the natural shape of the toes, accommodating the downward slope from big toe to little toe. It also creates a proper left and right sock so you have a genuine matching pair of socks.

Pros: This type of toe shaping provides the knitter with the opportunity to get a custom fit for the toe of your socks. There is plenty of room for the big toe and it adds the rounded shaping for the rest of the toes.

Con: You have to pay close to attention to your decreases/ increases and reverse them for the other sock. Taking notes is very important. Even though you are knitting a left sock and a right sock you want the angle of the slope to match.

Working Top Down

When you start the toe, the right-leaning and left-leaning decreases will only take place on one side of the sock to form the anatomical shaping as follows.

RIGHT FOOT DECREASES

Needle 1/Front Cable: K1, ssk, knit to end.

Needle 2/Back Cable: Knit to 3 sts before end, k2tog, k1.

LEFT FOOT DECREASES

Needle 1/Front Cable: Knit to 3 sts before end, k2tog, k1.

Needle 2/Back Cable: K1, ssk, knit to end.

The final toe decreases will take place on both sides of the sock, every round, to balance the shaping and are the same for both feet.

Top Down Anatomical Toe Instructions

Round 1: Work Left Foot or Right Foot Decreases depending on which sock you are knitting. 2 sts decreased.

Round 2: Knit all sts.

Repeat Rounds 1 & 2 a total of 10 times (20 rounds total), then continue to the final toe decreases.

Toe Decrease Shaping Round (same for both feet): K1, ssk, knit to last 3 sts of Needle 1, k2tog, k1. On Needle 2, k1, ssk, knit to last 3 sts, k2tog, k1. 4 sts decreased.

Repeat the Toe Decrease Shaping Round every round until the stitch count is 20 stitches total (10 on each needle).

Finish by grafting the remaining sts together (see Finish Line: Grafting Made Easy).

Working Toe Up

The first toe increases will take place on both sides of the sock, every round, to balance the shaping and are the same for both feet.

After the initial increases, right and left increases will only take place on one side of the sock as follows.

RIGHT FOOT INCREASES

Needle 1/Front Cable: K1, M1R, knit to the end of Needle 1.

Needle 2/Back Cable: Knit to 1 st before end, M1L, k1.

LEFT FOOT INCREASES

Needle 1/Front Cable: Knit to 1 st before end of Needle 1, M1L, k1.

Needle 2/Back Cable: K1, M1R, knit to end.

Toe Up Anatomical Toe Instructions

Using the cast on of your choice, cast on 20 stitches (10 on each needle).

Toe Increase Shaping Round (same for both feet): K1, M1R, knit to last st of Needle 1, M1L, k1. On Needle 2, k1, M1R, knit to last st, M1L, k1. 4 sts increased.

Repeat the Toe Increase Shaping Round a total of 6 (7) (9) times until you have 44 (48) (56) sts.

Round 1: Work Left Foot or Right Foot Increases depending on which sock you are knitting. 2 sts increased.

Round 2: Knit all sts.

Repeat Rounds 1 & 2 until you have 56 (64) (72) sts.

Rearrange the stitches as you prefer for your needles before beginning the foot.

CHAPTER EIGHT

Finish Line

"Knit on with confidence and hope through all crises"

ELIZABETH ZIMMERMANN

What's Left?

There are just the last finishing touches to do before you can don your socks and do a happy dance with warm, cozy feet!

GRAFTING MADE EASY

Grafting is a technique used to weave the front and back stitches of the toe together to close the sock when working from the top down. It has also been described as sewing in a row of stitches to, as we said, close the toe. This technique also makes the knitting look like it's "rolling" over the toe of the sock. It looks completely seamless.

If you are on Team Top Down and once you have finished knitting the toe, cut the yarn to a length three times as long as the width of the toe. You will now start weaving the stitches together with a tapestry (darning) needle.

There are two methods that I use and, in my experience, there is no need for a set up round. Simply starting weaving.

Grafting Method 1

Needle 1/Front needle:

Insert the tapestry (darning) needle into the first stitch as if to knit (A), slip the stitch off (B).

Insert the tapestry needle into the next stitch as if to purl (C), leave the stitch on (D).

Needle 2/Back needle:

Insert the tapestry needle into the first stitch as if to purl (E), slip the stitch off.

Insert the tapestry needle into the next stitch as if to knit, leave the stitch on (F).

Repeat until all the stitches have been removed from the needles, then insert the tapestry needle into the sock and weave in the tail.

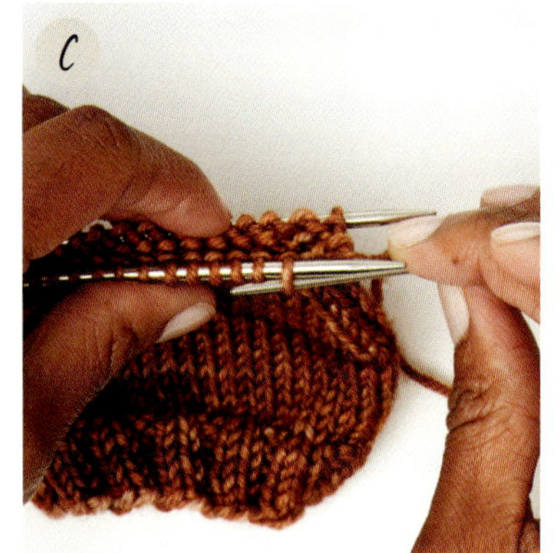

Grafting Method 2

Needle 1/Front needle:

Insert the tapestry (darning) needle into the first stitch as if to knit (A), slip the stitch off (but don't pull the yarn through). Insert the tapestry needle in the next stitch as if to purl (B).

Needle 2/Back needle:

Insert the tapestry needle in the first stitch as if to purl (C), slip the stitch off (but don't pull the yarn through). Insert the tapestry needle in the next stitch as if to knit (D).

Repeat until all the stitches have been removed from the needles, then insert the tapestry needle into the sock and weave in the tail.

JENY'S SURPRISINGLY STRETCHY BIND OFF

Toe up socks require a very stretchy bind (cast) off to ensure that your sock will fit over your foot. In my experience Jeny's Surprisingly Stretchy Bind Off truly is the best way to accomplish this. Once you get into the rhythm of the direction of the yarn overs your socks will be finished in no time.

Bind (cast) off your stitches in patten, 2x2 rib as follows:

1. Knit the first stitch.

2. Using a reverse yarn over (RYO), bring the yarn to the front by taking it over the right needle and then through the needles to the back again (A). Knit the next stitch. There are now 3 stitches on the right needle.

3. Lift the 2 stitches over the stitch nearest to the right needle tip to bind (cast) off (B). This leaves one stitch on the right needle.

4. Now bring the yarn to the front and around the needle (C) to create the next yarn over, then purl the next stitch.

5. Lift the 2 stitches over the first stitch to bind (cast) off, again leaving one stitch on the right needle. Yarn over in the same way, purl the next stitch, lift the 2 stitches over the first stitch and leaving one stitch on the right needle again.

6. Continue in this way, working a reverse yarn over before every knit stitch and a normal yarn over before every purl stitch until all the stitches are bound (cast) off except one remaining on the right needle.

7. Lengthen the last loop on your needle (D) and cut the working yarn.

8. Thread the yarn onto a tapestry (darning) needle and thread it from the back to the front through the first bound-off (cast-off) stitch (E). Pull the tapestry needle through the long loop and gently pull to join the stitches of the round. Thread the needle down through the center of the next bound-off stitch and to the inside of your sock.

8. Weave the yarn around the right leg of 2–3 more stitches, then cut your tail. This creates a very stretchy edge (F).

Keep in mind this bind (cast) off uses quite a bit of yarn because of the yarn overs, so make sure you have enough yarn remaining after knitting the leg of your sock. You should leave at least four times the circumference of the sock for binding (casting) off and weaving in the end.

A

B

C

D

E

F

Should I Wash My Socks?

Yes, you should wash your socks when needed, and by hand. I don't suggest machine washing unless it has a gentle/delicate wash cycle, and even then there is a risk your knitwear may be damaged. Play it safe and wash by hand.

Using a wool wash is best since it is designed to gently lift the dirt from your socks without the need for vigorous scrubbing. The water temperature should be lukewarm/ room temperature. The warmer the water the greater chance of shrinkage. And please don't scrub your socks like you might a pair of jeans. My mum used to use a washboard and very hot water. That combination would absolutely lead to felting and shrinkage of a knitted item.

To wash your socks, simply fill a basin or sink with lukewarm water, submerge your socks until saturated and let them sit. The dirtier the socks the darker the water. When using a wool wash there is no need to rinse the socks. Roll your socks in a towel or use a salad spinner (I learned that trick from Susan B. Anderson and the kids can help, they love it), then lay flat to dry. Make sure to get as much of the water out as possible because the weight of the excess water can distort the socks.

TO BLOCK OR NOT TO BLOCK?

I am going to be completely honest here and say if you are washing a plain vanilla sock with no texture or colorwork then simply washing them is enough!

If your sock has a textured design like cables or contains a colorwork pattern then absolutely yes, block your socks.

Blocking can right many "wrongs" in a sock. It can even out stitches, smooth out a colorwork pattern, add a bit of length or width if needed, as well as make your sock look "cleaner" in appearance.

Sock blockers are very useful and less troublesome then pinning your socks to the desired measurements. Sock blockers come in different sizes based on average foot lengths. They can be made of plastic, metal or wood. I like using ornate wooden blockers for pictures and display, and prefer metal blockers for actual blocking.

Metal blockers are usually just a frame in the shape of a sock. This allows air to flow easily and dries your socks more quickly.

I suggest putting the sock on the blocker, lightly spray it with water from a spray bottle or mister, or even a steamer (this is my favorite method). Then let the sock dry completely.

Don't over-wet your socks because this can stretch them out of shape and make them too loose to wear — yes, I speak from experience on this one.

CHAPTER NINE

Tips & Tricks

"Recipes tell you nothing. Learning techniques is the key"

TOM COLICCHIO

How Can I Improve?

Knitting socks gives you so many new skills to practice. Here's a few things I've learned along the way. Some of these skills I've learned from knitting other garments and working in a yarn shop, others out of necessity.

WINDING YARN

Yarn comes in a few different forms, balls, skeins, and hanks. No matter the "packaging" of the yarn I always wind it into "a cake". A cake of yarn is the shape it takes when a yarn winder is used. It is stable and won't roll away when in use.

When I wind yarn on a yarn winder I do it twice. WHY? Because there is usually some "tension" in the yarn when wound the first time. The yarn is stretched a bit, making the cake dense and tight. If left this way for too long the yarn can lose its elasticity. So I wind it a second time and the result is a bigger, fluffier cake that still holds its shape but maintains the quality of the yarn. It's a bit time consuming but so worth it.

cake wound once cake wound twice

cake wound once cake wound twice

AVOIDING LADDERS

Gaps also known as "ladders" occur when there is too much space between stitches. The most common place for this to happen is at the intersection between needles (A).

The easiest way to avoid this from happening is to overlap your needles. With the yarn coming from the back needle, place that needle UNDER the front needle (the one you are knitting with) and give a slight tug on the yarn (B).

Knit the first stitch (C), then as you are knitting the second stitch, give the working yarn a gentle pull (D) before completing the stitch (E). This will help the gap between the needles disappear (F).

Do this at the beginning of every needle change/intersection. Trust me if becomes a habit very quickly.

LADDERS DO NOT USUALLY FORM IF KNITTING WITH ONE SHORT CIRCULAR NEEDLE.

CHANGING COLORS AND AVOIDING "THE JOG"

How do you avoid the staggered look at the beginning of the round when changing color?

At the beginning of the round, start the new color and knit around to the last stitch.

When you start the next round, with the tip of the right needle, pick up the right leg of the stitch below the new color (A) and place it on the left needle (B). Knit it together with the first stitch (C).

By knitting the two stitches together you have "raised" the previous color up to match other new and "hidden" the jog one behind the other (D).

ADDING A DIFFERENT COLOR TO YOUR SOCK CUFF, HEEL AND TOE NOT ONLY PERSONALIZES THE PATTERN BUT ALSO ADDS A BEAUTIFUL POP OF COLOR TO YOUR SOCKS.

RIBBING AND THE DREADED "BLIP OF COLOR"

When changing color in ribbing or starting a ribbing section in a different color, there is a very simple way to eliminate those "blips" of color that appear in the purl stitches.

At the beginning of the round, start the new color and knit around to the last stitch. In the next round return to (or begin with) ribbing. Do note that this works best for stripes that are four or more rows wide.

MATCHING STRIPES

I'm obsessed with self-striping yarn and have a few tips to easily get a pair of matching socks — though there is nothing wrong with a "fraternal twin" pair of socks either.

Most dyers sell their yarn in one long skein. Once wound you can simply start knitting, making a note of the color you started and ended in order to knit the second sock to match. Other dyers sell their yarn in two matching skeins.

If using one skein, weigh the yarn and divide it evenly into two cakes, making sure to cut/break the yarn at the start of a color repeat. (Self-striping yarn can come in two, four, or as many as 24 color stripe repeats.)

If using two skeins, after winding hold a strand from each cake together, measure out the amount you need for the cast on you are using (A), put in a slip knot in the same spot on each strand (B), then start knitting. The slip knot on the second cake will ensure that your stripes will match perfectly.

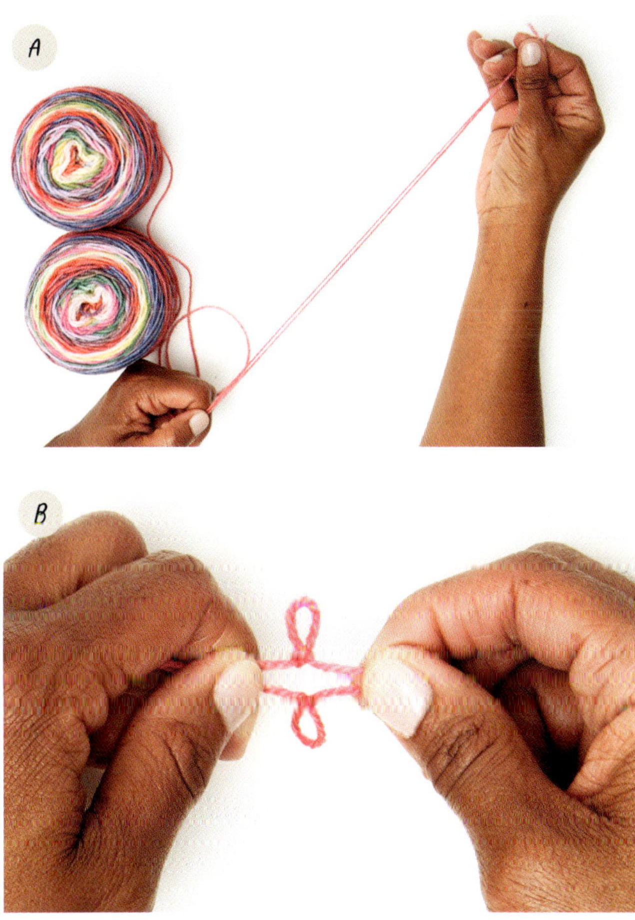

WEAVING IN ENDS AS YOU GO

One of the main reasons knitters don't like changing colors when knitting socks is to avoid weaving in all those loose ends when finished. Having the skill to weave, or rather knit, in your ends as you go is a game changer. And guess what, this can be applied to other projects and garments not just socks!

1. Knit to the end of the round with the old color (A). Break the yarn, leaving a tail about 6–8in/15–20.5cm long.

2. Bring the old yarn in front of the right needle (B). Now hold the old color in your left hand and the new color in you right hand (C).

3. Knit the first stitch with the new color (D), then knit the second stitch with the new color (E).

4. Bring the old yarn in front of the right needle (F) and knit the next stitch with the new color (G).

5. Repeat these steps for about 5–7 stitches. This is creating an "over/under" effect which is trapping the old color behind the new color along the inside of the sock (H).

6. Continue knitting with the new color until 6 stitches before the end of the round (I). Now we must weave in the starting tail of the new color.

7. Pass the tail of the new color between the 6th and 7th stitches before the end of the round (J). Slip your finger under the tail and bring it in front of the right needle (K).

8. Knit the stitch with the new color, then knit the next stitch (L).

9. Bring the yarn in front of the right needle and knit the stitch with the new color. Repeat in the same way to the end of the round (M). Note: it does not matter whether you end with the yarn in front or behind.

10. Now look to the inside of the sock (N). You will see two tails neatly woven into the wrong side of the sock. Gently pull on each tail, one at a time. This will even out the stitches and close any holes or gaps.

Your tails are woven in and you are free to happily continue knitting.

CHAPTER TEN

Patterns

"Comparison is the thief of joy"

THEODORE ROOSEVELT

PATTERN ONE

No Fear Shorty Socks

Afraid of knitting socks? Then start here! This easy shorty sock pattern is designed for the beginner (and fun for the experienced sock knitter too). Once you replace the fear with understanding, you will be knitting pair after pair in no time.

SKILL LEVEL

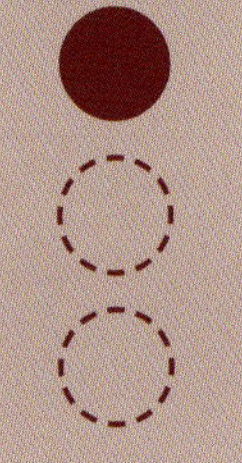

Sock Construction

Top down, shorty length, 2x2 rib cuff, stockinette (stocking stitch) leg and foot, top down heel flap and turn, round toe.

Sizes

Small (Medium) (Large).

Approximate foot circumference: 7in/17cm (8in/20cm) (9in/23cm).

Leg and foot lengths vary depending on the knitter's preference.

TAKE YOUR TIME AND READ THROUGH THE WHOLE PATTERN BEFORE YOU BEGIN.

Supplies List

YARN

Fingering (4ply) weight, approximately 400–450yd/370–420m.

Sample in Legacy Fiber Artz, Tea for Two colorway on Steel Toes base (75% Superwash Merino/25% Nylon), 100g, 463yd/423m.

NEEDLES

US 1 (2.25mm) or size required to obtain the gauge (tension).

NOTIONS

Removable stitch markers, tapestry (darning) needle, scissors.

Gauge (Tension)

32 stitches and 40 rounds per 4in/10cm in stockinette (stocking stitch).

ABBREVIATIONS

BOR	Beginning of round
K	Knit
Knitwise	Insert needle into stitch as if to knit (this moves a slipped stitch from left to right needle with a twist)
K2tog	Knit 2 stitches together
P	Purl
Purlwise	Insert needle into stitch as if to purl (this moves a slipped stitch from left to right needle without a twist)
P2tog	Purl 2 stitches together
RS	Right side
Sl	Slip stitch. Pattern will note if the stitch is to be slipped knitwise or purlwise. Unless noted, slip stitches with yarn in back of work
SSK	Slip, Slip, Knit
St(s)	Stitch(es)
Stockinette (stocking stitch)	Knit all stitches when working in the round. When working back and forth, knit on right side rows and purl on wrong side rows
WS	Wrong side
WYIF	With yarn held in front of work

INSTRUCTIONS

Cast on 56 (64) (72) sts using Long Tail Cast On. Being careful not to twist sts, join for working in the round. Place a marker to indicate BOR.

Cuff

Work 15 rounds of 2x2 rib, or cuff of your choice to desired length.

Leg

Knit 15 rounds in stockinette (stocking stitch) or to desired length.

Heel Flap (Slip Stitch)

Your heel flap will be worked flat across the first half of the sts, 28 (32) (36) sts. Arrange the sts so that the heel sts are easily worked back and forth.

Row 1 (RS): Sl 1 purlwise, (k1, sl 1 knitwise) to last st, k1.

Row 2 (WS): Sl 1 purlwise, purl to last st, k1.

Row 3 (RS): Sl 1 purlwise wyif, (k1, sl 1 knitwise) to last st, k1.

Row 4 (WS): Sl 1 purlwise, purl to last st, k1.

Repeat Rows 3 & 4 another 12 (14) (16) times.

You will have a total of 28 (32) (36) rows and a total of 14 (16) (18) slipped sts along each side of the heel flap.

Heel Turn

Row 1 (RS): Sl 1 purlwise, k16 (18) (20), ssk, k1, turn work.

Row 2 (WS): Sl 1 purlwise, p7, p2tog, p1, turn.

Row 3 (RS): Sl 1 purlwise, knit to 1 st before gap created by turn on previous row, ssk to close gap (using 1 st from each side of the gap), k1, turn.

Row 4 (WS): Sl 1 purlwise, purl to 1 st before gap created by turn on previous row, p2tog to close gap (using 1 st from each side of gap), p1, turn.

Repeat Rows 3 & 4 until all sts have been worked. You will end with a completed wrong side row and have 18 (20) (22) sts.

Gusset

Knit across the first 9 (10) (11) sts of the heel sts and move the BOR marker here at the center of the heel. There is no need to rearrange sts, just make a note of the shift.

Knit across the remaining 9 (10) (11) sts of the heel.

Pick up and knit 1 st in each of the 14 (16) (18) slipped sts along the left side of the heel flap. Pick up 1 extra st between the heel flap sts and the instep sts. Place a marker.

Knit across the instep sts (front of the sock). Place a marker.

Pick up 1 extra st between the instep sts and the heel flap sts.

Pick up and knit 1 st in each of the 14 (16) (18) slipped sts along the right side of the heel flap. Knit to the BOR marker.

You will now begin decreasing to return to your original stitch count.

Round 1: Slip BOR marker, knit to 3 sts before the next marker, k2tog, k1, slip marker, knit across instep sts to the next marker, slip marker, k1, ssk, knit to end of round. 2 sts decreased.

Round 2: Knit all sts.

Repeat Rounds 1 & 2 until you have 56 (64) (72) sts.

Foot

Once you are back to your original stitch count, knit in stockinette (stocking stitch) until the foot length measures 1½in/3.5cm (1¾in/4.5cm) (2in/5cm) shorter than your desired length.

Toe

Set up row: Remove BOR marker and knit to next marker, which becomes the new BOR marker at the side of the foot.

Depending on how you are managing your sts on the needles, you may want to distribute the sts evenly so that Needle 1/front cable holds the sts for the instep/top of your foot and Needle 2/back cable holds the sts for the bottom/sole of your foot. Otherwise place another marker at the left side of the foot to divide the sts in half.

Round 1 (decrease round): K1, ssk, knit to the last 3 sts before marker or end of Needle 1, k2tog, k1, slip marker if using, k1, ssk, knit to the last 3 sts of round, k2tog, k1. 4 sts decreased.

Round 2: Knit all sts.

Repeat Rounds 1 & 2 until there are 40 sts remaining in total (20 sts on each needle).

Then repeat only Round 1 (decreasing every round) until there are 20 sts remaining in total (10 sts on each needle).

Finishing

Graft the remaining sts together. Weave in all ends. Knit your second sock.

Hand wash gently in cool water, dry flat and enjoy!

CONVERTING TO TOE UP?

Using Turkish Cast On, cast on 20 sts and work the toe up instructions for the Round toe to 56 (64) (72) sts.

Knit the foot to desired length, then work the Toe Up Heel Flap and Gusset heel.

Work the leg as instructed, then the cuff.

Bind (cast) off using Jeny's Surprisingly Stretchy Bind Off.

PATTERN TWO

Rising Up Socks

After much trial and error I have embraced the simplicity, functionality, and genuine joy of knitting socks toe up. This pattern has mirrored toe increases, a short row heel, and a super stretchy bind off. It's perfect for the beginner and seasoned knitter alike.

Sock Construction

Toe up, shorty length, round toe, stockinette (stocking stitch) foot and leg, shadow wrap short row heel, 2x2 rib cuff.

Sizes

Small (Medium) (Large).

Approximate foot circumference: 7in/17cm (8in/20cm) (9in/23cm).

Leg and foot lengths vary depending on the knitter's preference.

NEEDLE SIZES IN US NUMBERS AND MM MAY VARY FROM ONE NEEDLE BRAND TO ANOTHER.

Supplies List

YARN

Fingering (4ply) weight, approximately 350–420yd/320–390m.

Sample in Legacy Fiber Artz, Cuppa colorway on Steel Toes base (75% Superwash Merino/25% Nylon), 100g, 463yd/423m.

NEEDLES

US 1 (2.25mm) or size required to obtain the gauge (tension).

NOTIONS

Removable stitch markers, tapestry needle, scissors.

Gauge (Tension)

32 stitches and 40 rounds per 4in/10cm in stockinette (stocking stitch).

ABBREVIATIONS

BOR	Beginning of round
K	Knit
KFB	Knit front and back
P	Purl
RS	Right side
SKL	Slip, Knit, Lift
St(s)	Stitch(es)
Stockinette (stocking stitch)	Knit all stitches when working in the round. When working back and forth, knit on right side rows and purl on wrong side rows
Tr st	Triplet stitch
Tw st	Twin stitch
WS	Wrong side

INSTRUCTIONS

Using Judy's Magic Cast On, cast on 20 sts, with 10 sts on the top needle and 10 sts on the bottom needle.

Toe

Round 1: Knit all sts. Place a marker to indicate BOR.

Round 2: K1, kfb, knit to 2 sts before the end of the top needle, skl, k1, then k1, kfb, knit to 2 sts before the end of the bottom needle, skl, k1. 4 sts increased.

Repeat Round 2 only, until you have 40 sts in total (20 sts on each needle).

Then repeat Rounds 1 & 2 until you have 56 (64) (72) total sts. Rearrange sts to suit your needles.

Foot

Knit in stockinette (stocking stitch) until foot measures 2in/5cm (2¼in/5.5cm) (2½in/6.5cm) shorter than desired measurement from tip of your toe to the back of your heel.

ONE OF THE ADVANTAGES OF BEING TEAM TOE UP IS TRYING ON YOUR SOCK TO DECIDE HOW LONG YOU WANT TO MAKE THE LEG.

Heel (Shadow Wrap Short Rows)

The heel is worked across half of the sts, 28 (32) (36) sts. Arrange the sts so that the heel sts are easily worked back and forth.

FIRST HALF OF THE HEEL

Row 1 (RS): K27 (31) (35) sts, tw st in the next st, turn.

Row 2 (WS): P26 (30) (34) sts, tw st in the next st, turn.

Row 3 (RS): Knit to 1 st before the tw st, tw st in the next st, turn.

Row 4 (WS): Purl to 1 st before the tw st, tw st in the next st, turn.

Repeat Rows 3 & 4 until there are 9 (11) (13) tw sts on each side of the heel and 10 sts at the center of the heel.

SECOND HALF OF THE HEEL

Row 1 (RS): Knit to first tw st, knit both strands of the tw st together, tr st in the next tw st, turn.

Row 2 (WS): Purl to first tw st, purl both strands of the tw st together, tr st in the next tw st, turn.

Row 3 (RS): Knit to first tr st, knit all strands of tr st, tr st in next tw st, turn.

Row 4 (WS): Purl to first tr st, purl all strands of tr st, tr st in next tw st, turn.

Repeat Rows 3 & 4 until 1 tr st remains on each side of the heel.

Knit across the heel sts, knit the tr st. You will now return to knitting in the round. Knit across the instep sts to the BOR marker. You will knit the last tr st at the beginning of the next round.

Leg

Knit in stockinette (stocking stitch) until the foot measures 1½in/4cm shorter than desired length.

Cuff

Work 15 rounds of 2x2 rib, or work cuff of your choice to desired length.

Bind (cast) off using Jeny's Surprisingly Stretchy Bind Off or another stretchy bind off.

Finishing

Weave in all ends. Knit your second sock.

Hand wash gently in cool water, dry flat and enjoy!

CONVERTING TO TOP DOWN?

Cast on 56 (64) (72) sts using Long Tail Cast On.

Work 15 rounds of 2x2 rib for cuff, then work leg in stockinette (stocking stitch) to 6in/15cm or desired length.

Work Shadow Wrap Short Row Heel as instructed.

Work foot until 1½in/3.5cm (1¾in/4.5cm) (2in/5cm) shorter than desired length.

Work top down instructions for Round toe, then graft the remaining sts together.

PATTERN THREE

Fearless DK Socks

If small needles scare you but you still want to knit socks, this is the pattern for you since it uses DK (light worsted) weight yarn. This pattern allows plenty of customization too, so let your imagination move you away from fear and into your new favorite socks.

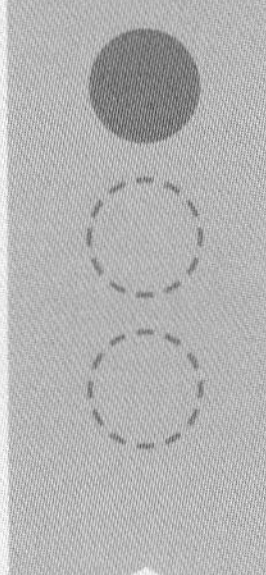

Sock Construction

Top down, shorty or full length, 2x2 rib cuff, stockinette (stocking stitch) leg and foot, shadow wrap short row heel, round toe.

Sizes

Small (Medium) (Large).

Approximate foot circumference: 7in/17cm (8in/20cm) (9¼in/23.5cm).

Leg and foot lengths vary depending on the knitter's preference.

HIGHLIGHT THE NUMBERS THAT APPLY TO THE SIZE YOU ARE KNITTING THROUGHOUT THE PATTERN TO AVOID ANY CONFUSION.

Supplies List

YARN

DK weight, approximately 160–280yd/150–260m.

Sample in Legacy Fiber Artz, Spring Fling DK mini bundle colorway on DK base (75% Superwash Merino/25% Nylon), five skeins each 20g, 49yd/45m.

NEEDLES

US 3 (3.25mm) or size required to obtain the gauge (tension).

NOTIONS

Removable stitch markers, tapestry (darning) needle, scissors.

Gauge (Tension)

24 stitches and 36 rounds per 4in/10cm in stockinette (stocking stitch).

ABBREVIATIONS

BOR	Beginning of round
K	Knit
K2tog	Knit 2 stitches together
P	Purl
RS	Right side
SSK	Slip, Slip, Knit
St(s)	Stitch(es)
Stockinette (stocking stitch)	Knit all stitches when working in the round. When working back and forth, knit on right side rows and purl on wrong side rows
Tr st	Triplet stitch
Tw st	Twin stitch
WS	Wrong side

INSTRUCTIONS

Cast on 40 (48) (56) sts using Long Tail Cast On. Being careful not to twist sts, join for working in the round. Place a marker to indicate BOR.

Cuff

Work 10 rounds of 2x2 rib, or cuff of your choice to desired length.

Leg

Knit in stockinette (stocking stitch) until you have reached the desired length from the cast-on edge.

Full Length Sock: Knit 45 rounds, or to desired length.

Shorty Sock: Knit 5 rounds, or to desired length.

Heel (Shadow Wrap Short Rows)

The heel is worked across half of the sts, 20 (24) (28) sts. Arrange the sts so that the heel sts are easily worked back and forth.

FIRST HALF OF THE HEEL

Row 1 (RS): K19 (23) (27) sts, tw st in the next st, turn.

Row 2 (WS): P18 (22) (26) sts, tw st in the next st, turn.

Row 3 (RS): Knit to 1 st before the tw st, tw st in the next st, turn.

Row 4 (WS): Purl to 1 st before the tw st, tw st in the next st, turn.

Repeat Rows 3 & 4 until there are 7 (8) (9) tw sts on each side of the heel and 6 (8) (10) sts at the center of the heel.

SECOND HALF OF THE HEEL

Row 1 (RS): Knit to first tw st, knit both strands of the tw st together, tr st in the next tw st, turn.

Row 2 (WS): Purl to first tw st, purl both strands of the tw st together, tr st in the next tw st, turn.

Row 3 (RS): Knit to first tr st, knit all strands of tr st, tr st in next tw st, turn.

Row 4 (WS): Purl to first tr st, purl all strands of tr st, tr st in next tw st, turn.

Repeat Rows 3 & 4 until 1 tr st remains on each side of the heel.

Knit across the heel sts, knit the tr st. You will now return to knitting in the round. Knit across the instep sts to the BOR marker. You will knit the last tr st at the beginning of the next round.

Foot

Knit in stockinette (stocking stitch) until the foot length measures 1½in/3.5cm (1¾in/4.5cm) (2in/5cm) shorter than your desired length.

Toe

Depending on how you are managing your sts on the needles, you may want to distribute the sts evenly so that Needle 1/front cable holds the sts for the instep/top of your foot and Needle 2/back cable holds the sts for the bottom/sole of your foot. Otherwise place another marker at the left side of the foot to divide the sts in half.

The beginning of the round should be at one side of the sock.

Round 1 (decrease round): K1, ssk, knit to the last 3 sts before marker or end of Needle 1, k2tog, k1, slip marker if using, k1, ssk, knit to the last 3 sts of round, k2tog, k1. 4 sts decreased.

Round 2: Knit all sts.

Repeat Rounds 1 & 2 until there are 20 (24) (28) sts remaining in total (10 (12) (14) sts on each needle).

Then repeat only Round 1 (decreasing every round) until there are 12 sts remaining in total (6 sts on each needle).

Finishing

Graft the remaining sts together. Weave in all ends. Knit your second sock.

Hand wash gently in cool water, dry flat and enjoy!

CONVERTING TO TOE UP?

Using Turkish Cast On, cast on 10 (12) (14) sts and work the toe up instructions for the Round toe to 40 (48) (56) sts.

Knit the foot to desired length, then work the Shadow Wrap Short Row Heel as instructed.

Work the leg as instructed, then the cuff.

Bind (cast) off using Jeny's Surprisingly Stretch Bind Off.

PATTERN FOUR

Soxploration Socks

I designed this simple vanilla sock pattern to help the beginner expand their skills and explore short row heels. It's just as enjoyable for experienced knitters looking for a relaxing project.

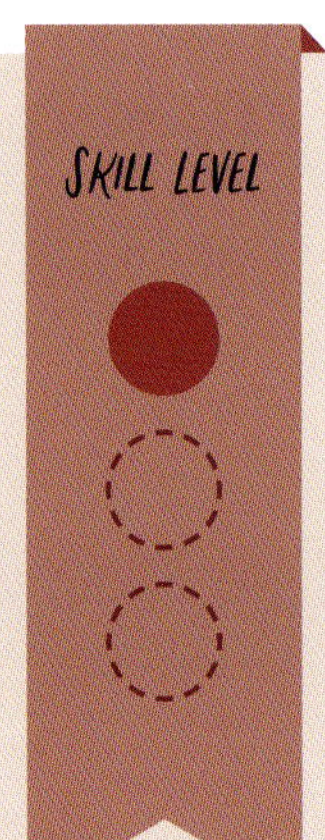

Sock Construction

Top down, shorty or full length, 2x2 rib cuff, stockinette (stocking stitch) leg and foot, shadow wrap short row heel, round toe.

Sizes

Small (Medium) (Large).

Approximate foot circumference: 7in/17cm (8in/20cm) (9in/23cm).

Leg and foot lengths vary depending on the knitter's preference.

SELF-STRIPING YARN LOOKS AMAZING WITH THIS SOCK DESIGN. I LIKE TO PAIR IT WITH A MATCHING SOLID FOR THE CUFF, TOE AND HEEL.

Supplies List

YARN

Fingering (4ply) weight, 400–450yd/370–420m.

Sample in The Cozy Knitter, in Season of Love colorway on Bliss base (80% Superwash Merino/20% Nylon), 115g, 413yd/378m.

NEEDLES

US 1 (2.25mm) or size required to obtain the gauge (tension).

NOTIONS

Removable stitch markers, tapestry (darning) needle, scissors.

Gauge (Tension)

32 stitches and 40 rounds per 4in/10cm in stockinette (stocking stitch).

ABBREVIATIONS

BOR	Beginning of round
K	Knit
K2tog	Knit 2 stitches together
P	Purl
RS	Right side
SSK	Slip, Slip, Knit
St(s)	Stitch(es)
Stockinette (stocking stitch)	Knit all stitches when working in the round. When working back and forth, knit on right side rows and purl on wrong side rows
Tr st	Triplet stitch
Tw st	Twin stitch
WS	Wrong side

INSTRUCTIONS

Cast on 56 (64) (72) sts using Long Tail Cast On. Being careful not to twist sts, join for working in the round. Place a marker to indicate BOR.

Cuff

Work 20 rounds of 2x2 rib, or cuff of your choice to desired length.

Leg

Knit in stockinette (stocking stitch) until you have reached your desired length.

Full Length Sock: Knit 50–60 rounds, or to desired length.

Shorty Sock: Knit 15–20 rounds, or to desired length.

Heel (Shadow Wrap Short Rows)

The heel can be worked using main color or, as seen in this version, using a contrast color across half of the sts, 28 (32) (36) sts. Arrange the sts so that the heel sts are easily worked back and forth.

FIRST HALF OF THE HEEL

Row 1 (RS): K27 (31) (35) sts, tw st in the next st, turn.

Row 2 (WS): P26 (30) (34) sts, tw st in the next st, turn.

Row 3 (RS): Knit to 1 st before the tw st, tw st in the next st, turn.

Row 4 (WS): Purl to 1 st before the tw st, tw st in the next st, turn.

Repeat Rows 3 & 4 until there are 9 (11) (13) tw sts on each side of the heel and 10 sts at the center of the heel.

SECOND HALF OF THE HEEL

Row 1 (RS): Knit to first tw st, knit both strands of the tw st together, tr st in the next tw st, turn.

Row 2 (WS): Purl to first tw st, purl both strands of the tw st together, tr st in the next tw st, turn.

Row 3 (RS): Knit to first tr st, knit all strands of tr st, tr st in next tw st, turn.

Row 4 (WS): Purl to first tr st, purl all strands of tr st, tr st in next tw st, turn.

Repeat Rows 3 & 4 until 1 tr st remains on each side of the heel.

Knit across the heel sts, knit the tr st. You will now return to knitting in the round. Knit across the instep sts to the BOR marker. You will knit the last tr st at the beginning of the next round.

Foot

Once you are back to your original stitch count, knit in stockinette (stocking stitch) until the foot length measures 1½in/3.5cm (1¾in/4.5cm) (2in/5cm) shorter than your desired length.

Toe

Depending on how you are managing your sts on the needles, you may want to distribute the sts evenly so that Needle 1/front cable holds the sts for the instep/top of your foot and Needle 2/back cable holds the sts for the bottom/sole of your foot. Otherwise place a marker at the left side of the foot to divide the sts in half.

Round 1 (decrease round): K1, ssk, knit to the last 3 sts before marker or end of Needle 1, k2tog, k1, slip marker if using, k1, ssk, knit to the last 3 sts of round, k2tog, k1. 4 sts decreased.

Round 2: Knit all sts.

Repeat Rounds 1 & 2 until there are 40 sts remaining in total (20 sts on each needle).

Then repeat only Round 1 (decreasing every round) until there are 20 sts remaining in total (10 sts on each needle).

Finishing

Graft the remaining sts together. Weave in all ends. Knit your second sock.

Hand wash gently in cool water, dry flat and enjoy!

IF USING A CONTRAST COLOR FOR CUFF, HEEL AND TOE, SIMPLY CHANGE COLORS AT THE START OF THESE SECTIONS THEN CHANGE TO THE MAIN COLOR FOR THE LEG AND FOOT.

CONVERTING TO TOE UP?

Using Judy's Magic Cast On, cast on 20 sts and work the toe up instructions for the Round toe to 56 (64) (72) sts.

Knit the foot to desired length, then work the Shadow Wrap Short Row Heel as instructed.

Work the leg as instructed, then the cuff.

Bind (cast) off using Jeny's Surprisingly Stretch Bind Off.

PATTERN FIVE

E3 Ankle Socks

My first knitting reference book was Elizabeth Zimmermann's *Knitting Without Tears*, which felt like reading a friend's knitting journal and reassured me that with a bit of practice I could be a skilled and happy knitter. This simple ankle sock is a tribute to her and her goal to help knitters knit without tears.

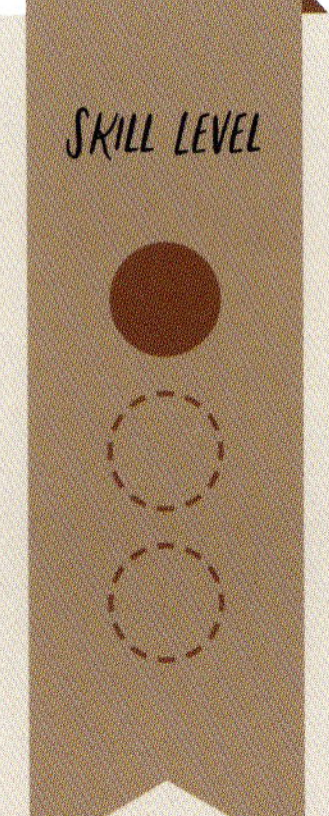

Sock Construction

Top down, ankle length (no leg), garter stitch cuff, top down heel flap and gusset, stockinette (stocking stitch) foot, round toe.

Sizes

Small (Medium) (Large).

Approximate foot circumference: 7in/17cm (8in/20cm) (9in/23cm).

Cuff and foot lengths vary depending on the knitter's preference.

THESE ANKLE SOCKS ARE VERY QUICK TO KNIT AND SUPER COMFY TO WEAR.

Supplies List

YARN
Fingering (4ply) weight, approximately 350–420yd/320–390m.

Sample in Knotty Pine Fiber Co., Another Glorious Morning colorway on Bighorn Sock base (80% Superwash Merino Wool, 20% Nylon), 100g, 400yd/366m.

NEEDLES
US 0 (2mm) and US 1 (2.25mm) or size required to obtain the gauge (tension).

NOTIONS
Removable stitch markers, tapestry (darning) needle, scissors.

Gauge (Tension)

32 stitches and 40 rounds per 4in/10cm in stockinette (stocking stitch).

ABBREVIATIONS

BOR	Beginning of round
Garter stitch	Alternate knit and purl rounds when working in the round. Two rounds create a garter "ridge"
K	Knit
Knitwise	Insert needle into stitch as if to knit (this moves a slipped stitch from left to right needle with a twist)
K2tog	Knit 2 stitches together
P	Purl
Purlwise	Insert needle into stitch as if to purl (this moves a slipped stitch from left to right needle without a twist)
P2tog	Purl 2 stitches together
RS	Right side
Sl	Slip stitch. Pattern will note if the stitch is to be slipped knitwise or purlwise. Unless noted, slip stitches with yarn in back of work
SSK	Slip, Slip, Knit
St(s)	Stitch(es)
Stockinette (stocking stitch)	Knit all stitches when working in the round. When working back and forth, knit on right side rows and purl on wrong side rows
WS	Wrong side
WYIF	With yarn held in front of work

INSTRUCTIONS

Using the smaller needles, cast on 56 (64) (72) sts using German Twisted Cast On (or cast on of your choice). Being careful not to twist sts, join for working in the round. Place a marker to indicate BOR.

Cuff

Knit in garter stitch for 10 rounds (5 ridges).

Change to the larger needles.

Knit one round.

Heel Flap (Slip Stitch)

Your heel flap will be worked flat across the first half of your sts, 28 (32) (36) sts. Arrange the sts so that the heel sts are easily worked back and forth.

Row 1 (RS): Sl 1 purlwise, (k1, sl 1 knitwise) to last st, k1.

Row 2 (WS): Sl 1 purlwise, purl to last st, k1.

Row 3 (RS): Sl 1 purlwise wyif, (k1, sl 1 knitwise) to last st, k1.

Row 4 (WS): Sl 1 purlwise, purl to last st, k1.

Repeat Rows 3 & 4 another 12 (14) (16) times.

You will have a total of 28 (32) (36) rows and a total of 14 (16) (18) slipped sts along each side of the heel flap.

Heel Turn

Row 1 (RS): Sl 1 purlwise, k16 (18) (20), ssk, k1, turn work.

Row 2 (WS): Sl 1 purlwise, p7, p2tog, p1, turn.

Row 3 (RS): Sl 1 purlwise, knit to 1 st before gap created by turn on previous row, ssk to close gap (using 1 st from each side of the gap), k1, turn.

Row 4 (WS): Sl 1 purlwise, purl to 1 st before gap created by turn on previous row, p2tog to close gap (using 1 st from each side of gap), p1, turn.

Repeat Rows 3 & 4 until all sts have been worked. You will end with a completed wrong side row and have 18 (20) (22) sts.

Gusset

Knit across the first 9 (10) (11) sts of the heel sts and then move the BOR marker to the center of the heel. There is no need to rearrange sts, just make a note of the shift.

Knit across the remaining 9 (10) (11) sts of the heel.

Pick up and knit 1 st in each of the 14 (16) (18) slipped sts along the left side of the heel flap. Pick up 1 extra st between the heel flap sts and the instep sts. Place a marker.

Knit across the instep sts (front of the sock). Place a marker.

Pick up 1 extra st between the instep sts and the heel flap sts.

Pick up and knit 1 st in each of the 14 (16) (18) slipped sts along the right side of the heel flap. Knit to the BOR marker.

You will now begin decreasing to return to your original stitch count.

Round 1: Slip BOR marker, knit to 3 sts before the next marker, k2tog, k1, slip marker, knit across instep sts to the next marker, slip marker, k1, ssk, knit to end of round. 2 sts decreased.

Round 2: Knit all sts.

Repeat Rounds 1 & 2 until you have 56 (64) (72) sts.

Foot

Once you are back to your original stitch count, knit in stockinette (stocking stitch) until the foot length measures 1½in/3.5cm (1¾in/4.5cm) (2in/5cm) shorter than your desired length.

Toe

Set up row: Remove BOR marker and knit to next marker, which becomes the new BOR marker at the side of the foot.

Depending on how you are managing your sts on the needles, you may want to distribute the sts evenly so that Needle 1/front cable holds the sts for the instep/top of your foot and Needle 2/back cable holds the sts for the bottom/sole of your foot. Otherwise place another marker at the left side of the foot to divide the sts in half.

Round 1 (decrease round): K1, ssk, knit to the last 3 sts before marker or end of Needle 1, k2tog, k1, slip marker if using, k1, ssk, knit to the last 3 sts of round, k2tog, k1. 4 sts decreased.

Round 2: Knit all sts.

Repeat Rounds 1 & 2 until there are 40 sts remaining in total (20 sts on each needle).

Then repeat only Round 1 (decreasing every round) until there are 20 sts remaining in total (10 sts on each needle).

Finishing

Graft the remaining sts together. Weave in all ends. Knit your second sock.

Hand wash gently in cool water, dry flat and enjoy!

CONVERTING TO TOE UP?

Using the larger needles and Judy's Magic Cast On, cast on 20 sts and work the toe up instructions for the Round toe to 56 (64) (72) sts.

Knit the foot to desired length, then work the Toe Up Heel Flap and Gusset heel.

Knit one round, then change to the smaller needles.

Knit in garter stitch for 10 rounds for the cuff.

Bind (cast) off using Jeny's Surprisingly Stretch Bind Off.

PATTERN SIX

Seeds of Color Socks

This is a great introduction to colorwork to experiment with, even if you've never tried it before. This very simple design alternates two contrasting colors to produce a beautiful seed-like pattern. Make sure to use two colors with high contrast.

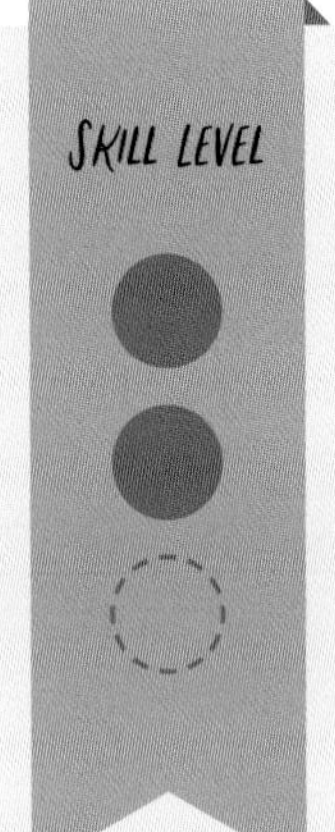

Sock Construction

Top down, full length, 2x2 rib cuff, simple colorwork leg, eye of partridge heel flap, heel turn, stockinette (stocking stitch) foot, round toe.

Sizes

Small (Medium) (Large).

Approximate foot circumference: 7in/17cm (8in/20cm) (9in/23cm).

Leg and foot lengths vary depending on the knitter's preference.

THE MAIN COLOR IS USED FOR THE CUFF AND FOOT, THE CONTRAST COLOR IS USED FOR THE HEEL AND TOE, AND BOTH COLORS ALTERNATE FOR THE COLORWORK LEG.

Supplies List

YARN

Fingering (4ply) weight in 2 contrasting colors, approximately 350–420yd/320–390m of main color and 130–140yd/120–130m of contrast color.

Sample in Legacy Fiber Artz, in Vanilla Bean (main) colorway and Sweatah Weathah (contrast) colorway on Steel Toes base (75% Superwash Merino/25% Nylon), 100g, 463yd/423m.

NEEDLES

US 1 (2.25mm) and US 2 (2.75mm) needles or size required to obtain the gauge (tension).

NOTIONS

Removable stitch markers, tapestry (darning) needle, scissors.

Gauge (Tension)

32 stitches and 40 rounds per 4in/10cm in stockinette (stocking stitch).

ABBREVIATIONS

BOR	Beginning of round
K	Knit
Knitwise	Insert needle into stitch as if to knit (this moves a slipped stitch from left to right needle with a twist)
K2tog	Knit 2 stitches together
P	Purl
Purlwise	Insert needle into stitch as if to purl (this moves a slipped stitch from left to right needle without a twist)
P2tog	Purl 2 stitches together
RS	Right side
Sl	Slip stitch. Pattern will note if the stitch is to be slipped knitwise or purlwise. Unless noted, slip stitches with yarn in back of work
SSK	Slip, Slip, Knit
St(s)	Stitch(es)
Stockinette (stocking stitch)	Knit all stitches when working in the round. When working back and forth, knit on right side rows and purl on wrong side rows
WS	Wrong side

WITH THE EYE OF PARTRIDGE PATTERN, THE SLIPPED STITCH IS OFFSET EVERY OTHER ROW. SOME SEE A DIAMOND, I SEE A NEST — WHICHEVER YOU SEE IT'S A BEAUTIFUL HEEL FLAP.

INSTRUCTIONS

Using the main color and smaller needles, cast on 56 (64) (72) sts using Long Tail Cast On. Being careful not to twist sts, join for working in the round. Place a marker to indicate BOR.

Cuff

With main color, work 10 rounds of 2x2 rib, or cuff of your choice to desired length.

Leg

Round 1: Change to larger needles and knit 1 plain round.

Round 2: Increase 1 st at the beginning of the round, then knit to the end of the round. 57 (65) (73) sts.

The colorwork pattern needs an odd number of sts so the same color does not meet at the end of the round.

Join contrast color at the beginning of the next round.

Round 3: (K1 with contrast color, k1 with main color) to last st, k1 with contrast color.

Round 4: (K1 with main color, k1 with contrast color) to last st, k1 with main color.

Repeat Rounds 3 & 4 until you have worked a total of 20 rounds in the colorwork pattern. Break contrast color.

Next round: Change to smaller needles and decrease 1 st at the beginning of the round, then knit to the end of the round. 56 (64) (72) sts.

Knit 9 more rounds in main color.

Heel Flap (Eye of Partridge)

I chose the Eye of Partridge heel flap because it compliments the colorwork pattern. The pattern is a 4-row repeat and creates a beautiful texture.

Your heel flap will be worked flat across the first half of the sts. 28 (32) (36) sts. Arrange the sts so that the heel sts are easily worked back and forth.

Join contrast color at start of next row.

Row 1 (RS): Sl 1 purlwise, (k1, sl 1 purlwise) to last st, k1.

Row 2 (WS): Sl 1 purlwise, purl across the row.

Row 3 (RS): Sl 1 purlwise, (sl 1 purlwise, k1) to last st, k1.

Row 4 (WS): Sl 1 purlwise, purl across the row.

Repeat these 4 rows until you have worked 28 (32) (34) rows in total.

Heel Turn

Row 1 (RS): Sl 1 purlwise, k16 (18) (20), ssk, k1, turn work.

Row 2 (WS): Sl 1 purlwise, p7, p2tog, p1, turn.

Row 3 (RS): Sl 1 purlwise, knit to 1 st before gap created by turn on previous row, ssk to close gap (using 1 st from each side of the gap), k1, turn.

Row 4 (WS): Sl 1 purlwise, purl to 1 st before gap created by turn on previous row, p2tog to close gap (using 1 st from each side of gap), p1, turn.

Repeat Rows 3 & 4 until all sts have been worked. You will end with a completed wrong side row and have 18 (20) (22) sts.

Gusset

Knit across the first 9 (10) (11) sts of the heel sts and move the BOR marker to the center of the heel. There is no need to rearrange sts, just make a note of the shift.

Knit across the remaining 9 (10) (11) sts of the heel.

With main color, pick up and knit 1 st in each of the 14 (16) (18) slipped sts along the left side of the heel flap. Pick up 1 extra st between the heel flap sts and the instep sts. Place a marker.

Knit across the instep sts (front of the sock). Place a marker. Pick up 1 extra st between the instep sts and the heel flap sts. Pick up and knit 1 st in each of the 14 (16) (18) slipped sts along the right side of the heel flap. Knit to the BOR marker.

You will now begin decreasing to return to your original stitch count.

Round 1: Slip BOR marker, knit to 3 sts before the next marker, k2tog, k1, slip marker, knit across instep sts to the next marker, slip marker, k1, ssk, knit to end of round. 2 sts decreased.

Round 2: Knit all sts.

Repeat Rounds 1 & 2 until you have 56 (64) (72) sts.

Foot

Once you are back to your original stitch count, knit in stockinette (stocking stitch) until the foot length measures 1½in/3.5cm (1¾in/4.5cm) (2in/5cm) shorter than your desired length.

Toe

Set up row: Remove BOR marker and knit to next marker, which becomes the new BOR marker at the side of the foot.

Place another marker at the left side of the foot to divide the sts in half.

Join contrast color at start of next round.

Round 1 (decrease round): K1, ssk, knit to the last 3 sts before marker or end of Needle 1, k2tog, k1, slip marker if using, k1, ssk, knit to the last 3 sts of round, k2tog, k1. 4 sts decreased.

Round 2: Knit all sts.

Repeat Rounds 1 & 2 until there are 40 sts remaining in total (20 sts on each needle).

Then repeat only Round 1 (decreasing every round) until there are 20 sts remaining in total (10 sts on each needle).

Finishing

Graft the remaining sts together. Weave in all ends. Knit your second sock.

Hand wash gently in cool water, dry flat and enjoy!

CONVERTING TO TOE UP?

Using the smaller needles and contrast color, use Judy's Magic Cast On to cast on 20 sts and work the toe up instructions for the Round toe to 56 (64) (72) sts.

Change to main color and knit the foot to desired length, then work the Toe Up Heel Flap and Gusset heel, working the gusset in main color and the heel turn and gusset in contrast color.

For the leg, change to main color and work 10 rounds, increasing 1 st at end of final round. Change to larger needles and repeat Rounds 3 & 4 of leg as instructed for top down sock. Break contrast color and decrease 1 st at start of next round, then knit 1 further round.

Change to the smaller needles and work cuff.

Bind (cast) off using Jeny's Surprisingly Stretch Bind Off.

PATTERN SEVEN

Helical Socks

This ingenious technique creates a seamless, jogless fabric with beautiful mini stripes. Once you get the hang of this method, you can experiment with two solid colors, a solid and a variegated, or solid and self-striping combinations.

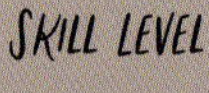

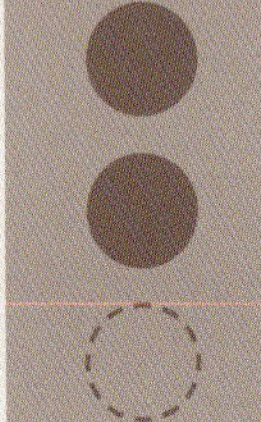

Sock Construction

Top down, full length, 2x2 rib cuff, stockinette (stocking stitch) leg and foot, shadow wrap short row heel, round toe.

Sizes

Small (Medium) (Large).

Approximate foot circumference: 7in/17cm (8in/20cm) (9in/23cm).

Leg and foot lengths vary depending on the knitter's preference.

THE MAIN COLOR IS USED FOR THE CUFF, HEEL AND TOE AND THE CONTRAST COLOR IS USED FOR THE STRIPES — BUT FEEL FREE TO MIX IT UP IN WHATEVER WAY YOU LIKE.

Supplies List

YARN

Fingering (4ply) weight in 2 contrasting colors, approximately 230–260yd/210–240m of each color.

Sample in Legacy Fiber Artz, in Vanilla Bean and Grey Gardens colorways on Steel Toes base (75% Superwash Merino/25% Nylon), 100g, 463yd/423m.

NEEDLES

US 1 (2.25mm) or size required to obtain the gauge (tension).

NOTIONS

Removable stitch markers, tapestry needle, scissors.

Gauge (Tension)

32 stitches and 40 rounds per 4in/10cm in stockinette (stocking stitch).

ABBREVIATIONS

BOR	Beginning of Round
K	Knit
K2tog	Knit 2 stitches together
P	Purl
Purlwise	Insert needle into stitch as if to purl (this moves a slipped stitch from left to right needle without a twist)
RS	Right side
SSK	Slip, Slip, Knit
St(s)	Stitch(es)
Stockinette (stocking stitch)	Knit all stitches when working in the round. When working back and forth, knit on right side rows and purl on wrong side rows
Tr st	Triplet stitch
Tw st	Twin stitch
WS	Wrong side

INSTRUCTIONS

Using the main color, cast on 56 (64) (72) sts using Long Tail Cast On. Being careful not to twist sts, join for working in the round. Place a marker to indicate BOR.

Cuff

Work 2x2 rib for 15 rounds (short version) or 20 rounds (long version).

Leg

At the beginning of the round, join the contrast color.

Knit to 3 sts before the main color, slip those 3 sts purlwise, pick up the main color and continue knitting.

You will continue knitting around stopping 3 sts before the color change until the leg of the sock is the desired length.

This is the way I knit my helical socks. Slipping the 3 sts moves the beginning of the round to the right. Changing from one color to the other in this way "offsets" the beginning of the round and eliminates a potential seam from forming.

Knitting right up to the next color can create what looks like a seam or line where the colors meet. There are different ways to avoid this – some knitters can control their gauge and it will not be apparent. For beginners, this offset method will ensure against a faux seam line anywhere on the sock.

And does it have to be 3 sts? No, it can be 2 or 4 — consistency is key. For this pattern I have chosen 3 sts.

Knit in stockinette (stocking stitch) until you have reached the desired length from the cast-on edge, ending with the main color.

Heel (Shadow Wrap Short Rows)

The heel can be worked using main color or, as seen in this version, using contrast color across half of the sts, 28 (32) (36) sts. Arrange the sts so that the heel sts are easily worked back and forth (see The Fun Part: Shadow Wrap Show Row Heel for how to manage the two yarns).

FIRST HALF OF THE HEEL

Row 1 (RS): K27 (31) (35) sts, tw st in the next st, turn.

Row 2 (WS): P26 (30) (34) sts, tw st in the next st, turn.

Row 3 (RS): Knit to 1 st before the tw st, tw st in the next st, turn.

Row 4 (WS): Purl to 1 st before the tw st, tw st in the next st, turn.

Repeat Rows 3 & 4 until there are 9 (11) (13) tw sts on each side of the heel and 10 sts at the center of the heel.

SECOND HALF OF THE HEEL

Row 1 (RS): Knit to first tw st, knit both strands of the tw st together, tr st in the next tw st, turn.

Row 2 (WS): Purl to first tw st, purl both strands of the tw st together, tr st in the next tw st, turn.

Row 3 (RS): Knit to first tr st, knit all strands of tr st, tr st in next tw st, turn.

Row 4 (WS): Purl to first tr st, purl all strands of tr st, tr st in next tw st, turn.

Repeat Rows 3 & 4 until 1 tr st remains on each side of the heel.

Knit across the heel sts, knit the tr st. You will now return to knitting in the round. Knit across the instep sts to the BOR marker. You will knit the last tr st at the beginning of the next round.

Foot

When you have finished the triple st on the right side of the heel continue with the main color until you are once again 3 sts before the contrast color. You will now continue knitting and changing colors in the same way you did on the leg.

The contrast color will be used to knit the remaining triple st on the other side of the heel.

Continue knitting helically as for the leg until the foot length measures 1½in/3.5cm (1¾in/4.5cm) (2in/5cm) shorter than your desired length, ending with the main color.

Toe

Set up row: Break the contrast color, then continue to knit with the main color to the BOR, making sure this is at the side of the foot.

Depending on how you are managing your sts on the needles, you may want to distribute the sts evenly so that Needle 1/front cable holds the sts for the instep/top of your foot and Needle 2/back cable holds the sts for the bottom/sole of your foot. Otherwise place another marker at the left side of the foot to divide the sts in half.

Round 1 (decrease round): K1, ssk, knit to the last 3 sts before marker or end of Needle 1, k2tog, k1, slip marker if using, k1, ssk, knit to the last 3 sts of round, k2tog, k1. 4 sts decreased.

Round 2: Knit all sts.

Repeat Rounds 1 & 2 until there are 40 sts remaining in total (20 sts on each needle).

Then repeat only Round 1 (decreasing every round) until there are 20 sts remaining in total (10 sts on each needle).

Finishing

Graft the remaining sts together. Weave in all ends. Knit your second sock.

Hand wash gently in cool water, dry flat and enjoy!

CONVERTING TO TOE UP?

Using Judy's Magic Cast On and the main color, cast on 20 sts and work the toe up instructions for the Round toe to 56 (64) (72) sts.

Follow the instructions given in the leg to start working helically and knit the foot to desired length, ending with the main color. Work the Shadow Wrap Short Row Heel as instructed.

Work the leg helically to desired length, ending with the main color, then work the cuff.

Bind (cast) off using Jeny's Surprisingly Stretch Bind Off.

PATTERN EIGHT

Alacrity Socks

This sock pattern explores the beauty, comfort, and durability of a garter stitch heel flap, square heel turn, and round toe. If you understand the basics of sock knitting and want to try something new, then this is the pattern for you.

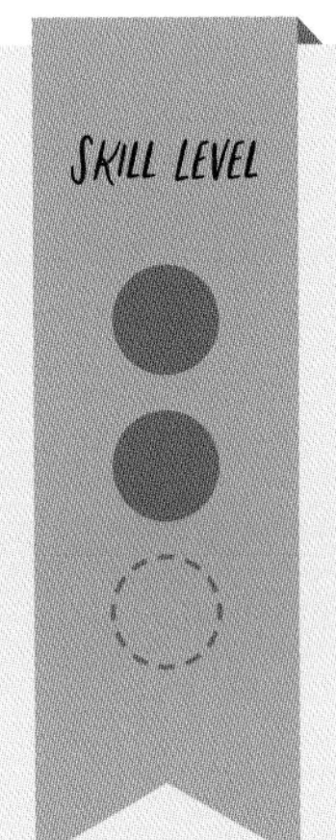

Sock Construction

Top down, full length, 2x2 rib cuff, stockinette (stocking stitch) leg and foot, garter stitch heel flap, square heel turn, garter stitch or stockinette (stocking stitch) round toe.

Sizes

Small (Medium) (Large).

Approximate foot circumference: 7in/17cm (8in/20cm) (9in/23cm).

Leg and foot lengths vary depending on the knitter's preference.

THE SQUARE HEEL, ALSO KNOWN AS THE DUTCH HEEL, MAINTAINS THE WIDTH OF THE TURNED HEEL FROM BEGINNING TO END AND HAS A SQUARED LOOK ONCE COMPLETED.

Supplies List

YARN

Fingering (4ply) weight, 400–475yd/370–435m.

Sample 1 in Woolens & Nosh, in So This Is Love colorway on SW Targhee base (90% Superwash Targhee/10% Nylon), 115g, 465yd/425m.

Sample 2 in Tiny Human Knits, in Carols In The Snow colorway on Basic Sock base (80% Superwash Merino/20% Nylon), 100g, 400yd/366m.

NEEDLES

US 1 (2.25mm) or size required to obtain the gauge (tension).

NOTIONS

Removable stitch markers, tapestry (darning) needle, scissors.

Gauge (Tension)

32 stitches and 40 rounds per 4in/10cm in stockinette (stocking stitch).

ABBREVIATIONS

BOR	Beginning of round
Garter stitch	Knit every row when working back and forth. Alternate knit and purl rounds when working in the round. Two rows/rounds create a garter "ridge"
K	Knit
Knitwise	Insert needle into stitch as if to knit (this moves a slipped stitch from left to right needle with a twist)
K2tog	Knit 2 stitches together
P	Purl
Purlwise	Insert needle into stitch as if to purl (this moves a slipped stitch from left to right needle without a twist)
P2tog	Purl 2 stitches together
RS	Right side
Sl	Slip stitch. Pattern will note if the stitch is to be slipped knitwise or purlwise. Unless noted, slip stitches with yarn in back of work
SSK	Slip, Slip, Knit
SSP	Slip, Slip, Purl
St(s)	Stitch(es)
Stockinette (stocking stitch)	Knit all stitches when working in the round. When working back and forth, knit on right side rows and purl on wrong side rows
Tbl	Through the back leg
WS	Wrong side
WYIF	With yarn held in front of work

INSTRUCTIONS

Cast on 56 (64) (72) sts using Long Tail Cast On. Being careful not to twist sts, join for working in the round. Place a marker to indicate BOR.

Cuff

Work 15 rounds of 2x2 rib, or cuff of your choice to desired length.

Leg

Knit 15 rounds in stockinette (stocking stitch) or to desired length.

Heel Flap (Garter Stitch)

Your heel flap will be worked flat across the first half of the sts, 28 (32) (36) sts. Arrange the sts so that the heel sts are easily worked back and forth.

Row 1 (RS): Sl 1 purlwise, knit to end of row.

Row 2 (WS): Sl 1 purlwise wyif, knit to end of row.

Repeat Rows 1 & 2 another 13 (15) (17) times.

You will have a total of 28 (32) (36) rows and a total of 14 (16) (18) slipped sts along each side of the heel flap.

Heel Turn (Garter Stitch or Stockinette/ Stocking Stitch)

The heel turn will be worked back and forth on either side of the central 10 (10) (12) heel sts, decreasing on every row.

The heel sts are distributed as follows:

Small (28 sts): 9 sts/10 sts/9 sts

Medium (32 sts): 11 sts/10 sts/11 sts

Large (36 sts): 12 sts/12 sts/12 sts

OPTION 1 – GARTER STITCH HEEL TURN

Row 1 (RS): Sl 1 purlwise, k17 (20) (23), k2tog, turn.

Row 2 (WS): Sl 1 purlwise, k8 (10) (12), k2tog, turn.

Row 3 (RS): Sl 1 purlwise, k8 (10) (12), k2tog, turn.

Repeat Rows 2 & 3 until all sts have been worked and 10 (10) (12) sts remain on the heel flap, ending after a Row 2.

OPTION 2 – STOCKINETTE (STOCKING STITCH) HEEL TURN

Row 1 (RS): Sl 1 purlwise, k17 (20) (23), k2tog, turn.

Row 2 (WS): Sl 1 purlwise, p8 (10) (12), p2tog, turn.

Row 3 (RS): Sl 1 purlwise, k8 (10) (12), k2tog, turn.

Repeat Rows 2 & 3 until all sts have been worked and 10 (10) (12) sts remain on the heel flap, ending after a Row 2.

Gusset

Round 1: Knit across the heel sts, place a marker, pick up and knit 1 st in each of the 14 (16) (18) slipped sts along the left side of the heel flap, pick up 1 extra st between the heel flap sts and the instep sts, place a marker, knit across the instep sts (front of the sock), place a marker, pick up 1 extra st between the instep sts and the heel flap sts, pick up and knit 1 st in each of the 14 (16) (18) slipped sts along the right side of the heel flap, place BOR at the right side of the heel.

Round 2: Knit across the heel sts to the next marker, remove marker, (k1 tbl) to 3 sts before the next marker, k2tog, k1 tbl, slip marker, work instep sts to next marker, slip marker, k1 tbl, ssk, (k1 tbl) to end of round.

Round 3: Knit all sts.

Round 4: Knit to 3 sts before the next marker, k2tog, k1, slip marker, knit across instep sts to the next marker, slip marker, k1, ssk, knit to end of round. 2 sts decreased.

Repeat Rounds 3 & 4 until you have 56 (64) (72) sts.

Foot

Remove the markers before and after the instep sts.

Once you are back to your original stitch count, knit in stockinette (stocking stitch) until the foot length measures 1½in/3.5cm (1¾in/4.5cm) (2in/5cm) shorter than your desired length.

Toe (Garter Stitch or Stockinette)

Depending on how you are managing your sts on the needles, you may want to distribute the sts evenly so that Needle 1/front cable holds the sts for the instep/top of your foot and Needle 2/back cable holds the sts for the bottom/sole of your foot. Otherwise place another marker at the left side of the foot to divide the sts in half.

OPTION 1 – GARTER STITCH TOE

Round 1 (decrease round): K1, ssk, knit to the last 3 sts before marker or end of Needle 1, k2tog, k1, slip marker if using, k1, ssk, knit to the last 3 sts of round, k2tog, k1. 4 sts decreased.

Round 2: Purl all sts.

Repeat Rounds 1 & 2 until there are 40 sts remaining in total (20 sts on each needle).

Round 3 (knit decrease round): K1, ssk, knit to the last 3 sts before marker or end of Needle 1, k2tog, k1, slip marker if using, k1, ssk, knit to the last 3 sts of round, k2tog, k1. 4 sts decreased.

Round 4 (purl decrease round): P1, ssp, purl to the last 3 sts before marker or end of Needle 1, p2tog, p1, slip marker if using, p1, ssp, purl to the last 3 sts of round, p2tog, p1.

4 sts decreased.

Repeat Rounds 3 & 4 (decreasing every round) until there are 20 sts remaining in total (10 sts on each needle).

OPTION 2 – STOCKINETTE TOE

Round 1 (decrease round): K1, ssk, knit to the last 3 sts before marker or end of Needle 1, k2tog, k1, slip marker if using, k1, ssk, knit to the last 3 sts of round, k2tog, k1. 4 sts decreased.

Round 2: Knit all sts.

Repeat Rounds 1 & 2 until there are 40 sts remaining in total (20 sts on each needle).

Then repeat only Round 1 (decreasing every round) until there are 20 sts remaining in total (10 sts on each needle).

Finishing

Graft the remaining sts together. Weave in all ends. Knit your second sock.

Hand wash gently in cool water, dry flat and enjoy!

CONVERTING TO TOE UP?

Using Judy's Magic Cast On, cast on 20 sts and work the toe up instructions for the Round toe to 56 (64) (72) sts in either garter stitch or stockinette (stocking stitch).

Knit the foot to desired length, then work the Toe Up Heel Flap and Gusset: Square Heel Option.

Work leg to desired length, then work the cuff.

Bind (cast) off using Jeny's Surprisingly Stretch Bind Off.

General Techniques

BASIC STITCHES

Slip Knot

The slip knot is like an anchor, marking the first stitch or holding the yarn in place. Make a loop crossing the working yarn over the tail end (A). Pull through another loop by pulling the working yarn through the first loop and place this on the needle (B). Lightly pull the tail to tighten the stitch on the needle (C).

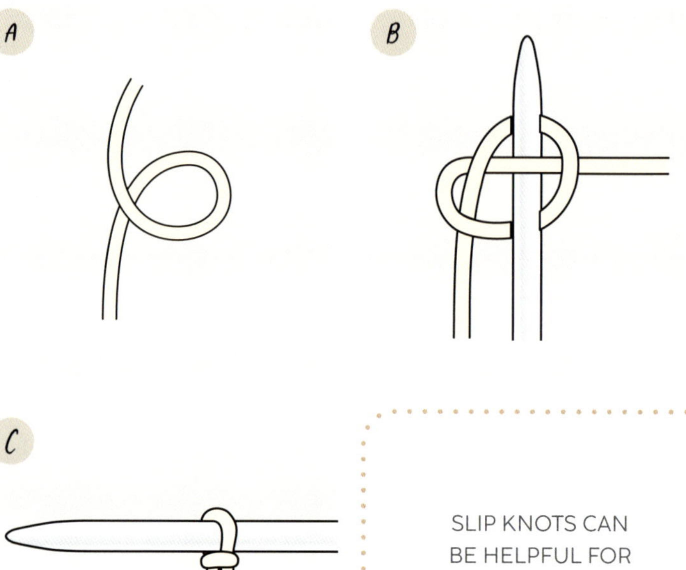

SLIP KNOTS CAN BE HELPFUL FOR MARKING YOUR PLACE ON A SECOND SKEIN TO MATCH STRIPES ON BOTH SOCKS.

Knit Stitch (K)

Hold the needle with the stitches in your left hand, with the yarn at the back. Insert the tip of the right needle into the first stitch from front to back and left to right (D). Take the yarn under and around the right needle from left to right (E). Use the tip of the right needle to pull the loop through the stitch on the left needle to form a new stitch on the right needle (F). Slide off the stitch on the left needle (G).

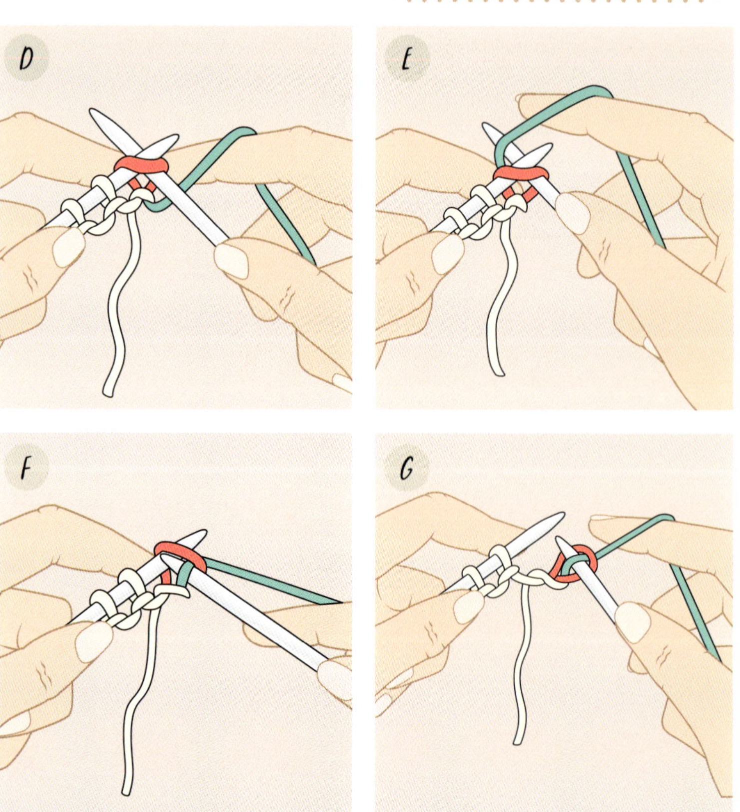

Purl Stitch (P)

Hold the needle with the stitches in your left hand, with the yarn at the front. Insert the tip of the right needle into the first stitch from right to left (H). Take the yarn over and around the right needle (I). Use the tip of the right needle to pull the loop through the stitch on the left needle to form a new stitch on the right needle (J). Slide off the stitch on the left needle (K).

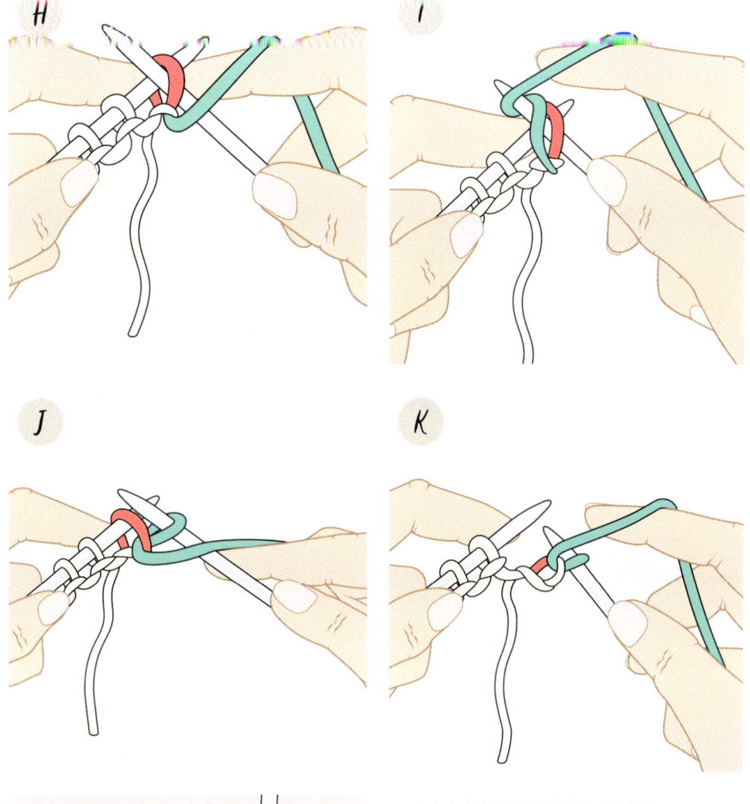

K1 tbl (Knit Through Back Leg)

Insert the right needle tip into the back leg of the next stitch from right to left (L). Wrap the yarn around the right needle as for a normal knit stitch.

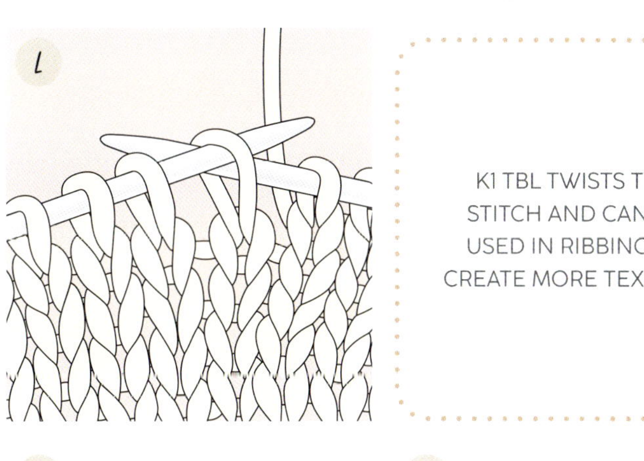

K1 TBL TWISTS THE STITCH AND CAN BE USED IN RIBBING TO CREATE MORE TEXTURE.

Pick Up and Knit

Insert the right needle from the front to the back into the slipped stitch along the row edge (M). Wrap the yarn around the needle as if to work a knit stitch, and then pull the loop on the needle through to the front of your knitting to create a new stitch (N).

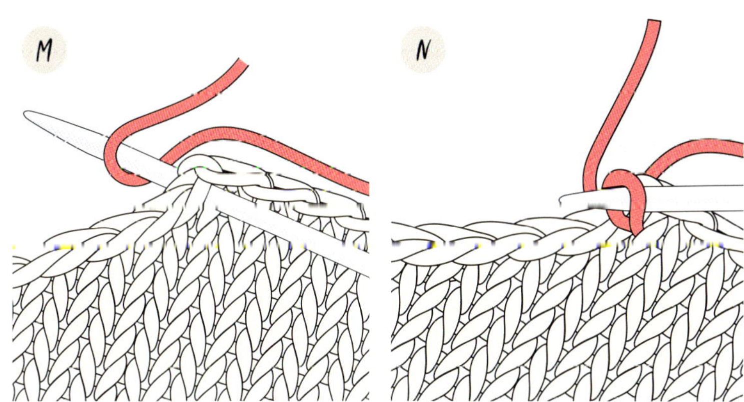

INCREASES

KFB: Knit Front and Back

Insert the tip of the right needle into the stitch and knit it in the usual way but do not slip it off the left needle. Insert the tip of the right needle into the back of the same stitch on the left needle and knit the stitch again (A). Now slip the original stitch off the left needle. This is a left-leaning bar increase.

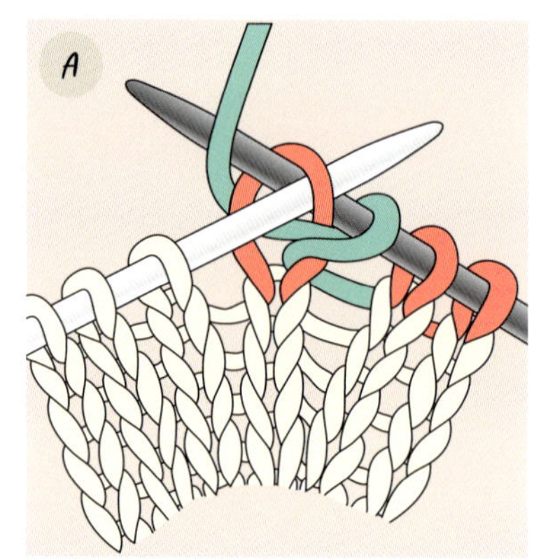

BAR INCREASES SHOW AS A SMALL HORIZONTAL LINE (A "BAR") ON THE FABRIC.

SKL: Slip, Knit, Lift

Slip one stitch knitwise (B). Slip the same stitch from the right to the left needle purlwise, maintaining the twist (C). Knit the stitch as normal (D). Lift the right leg of the stitch one row below the new stitch on the right needle to the left needle (E). Knit the loop on the left needle through the back leg (F). This is a right-leaning bar increase.

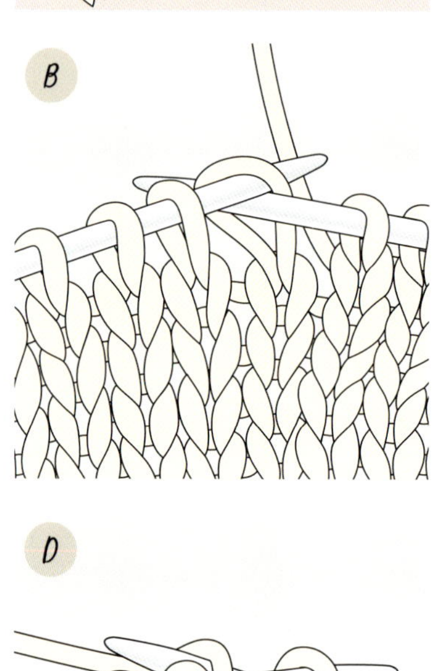

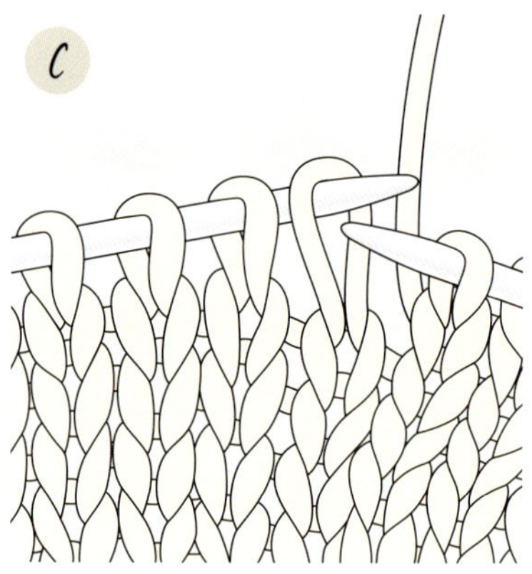

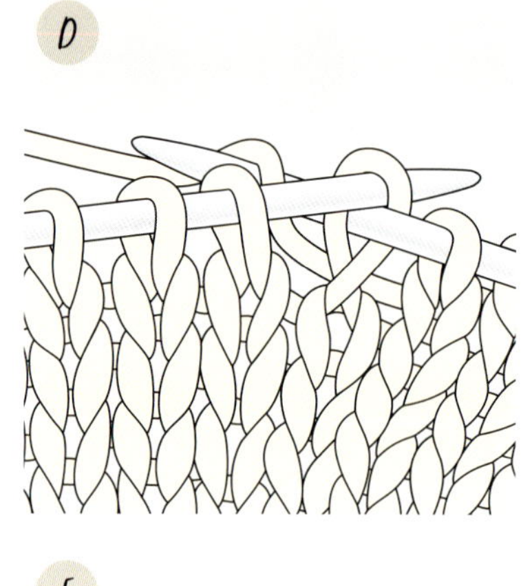

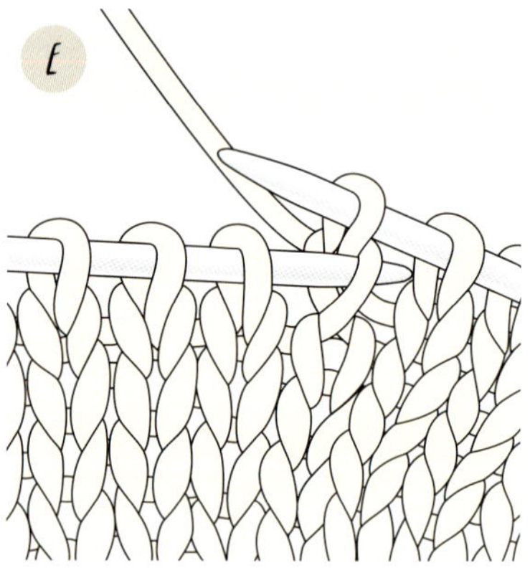

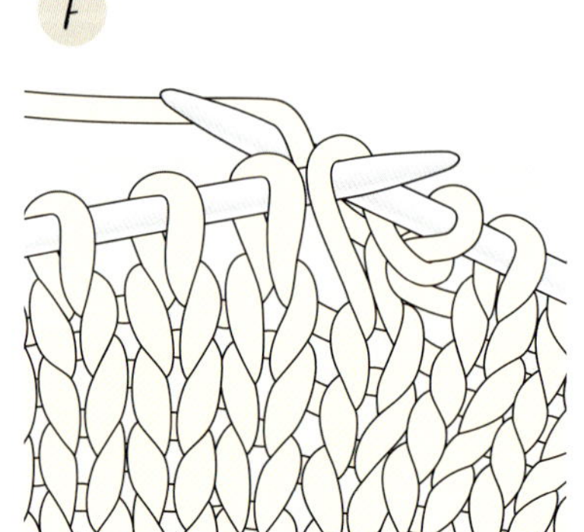

I LIKE TO PAIR SKL AND KFB INCREASES TOGETHER BECAUSE THEY MIRROR EACH OTHER.

YO: Yarn Over

Before working the next knit stitch, bring the yarn to front of the work in between the needles, and back over the right needle to the back of the work to create a stitch (G).

RYO: Reverse Yarn Over

Before working the next knit stitch, bring the yarn to the front by bringing it up over the right needle and then through the needles to the back of the work to create a stitch (H).

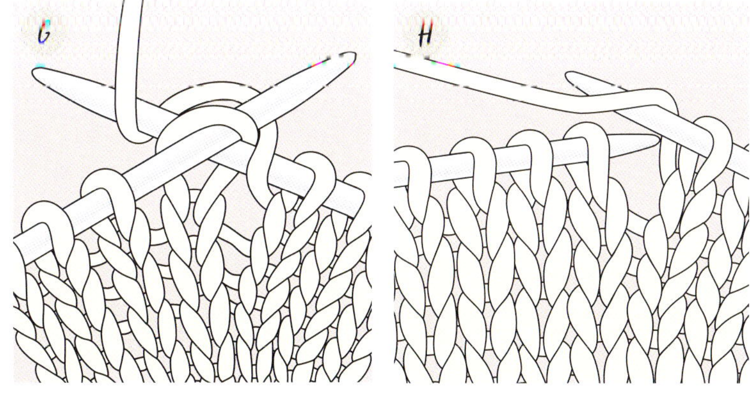

Make One Left (M1L)

Pick up the bar between two stitches (I), twist it and place on the left needle. Knit into the back leg (J) to increase by one stitch.

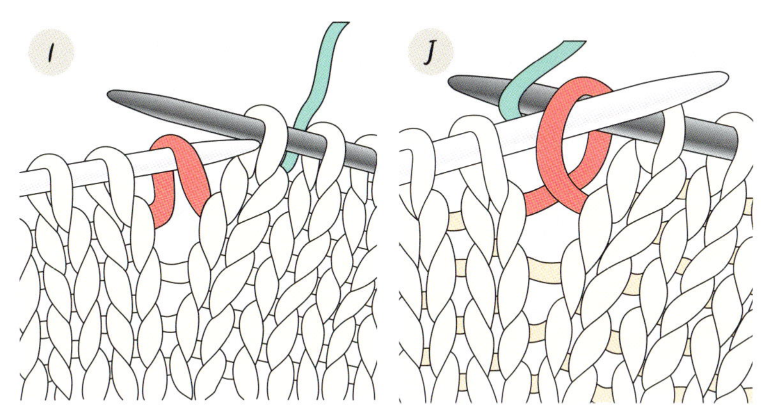

Make One Right (M1R)

Pick up the bar between two stitches (K), twist it and place on the left needle. Knit into the front loop (L) to increase by one stitch.

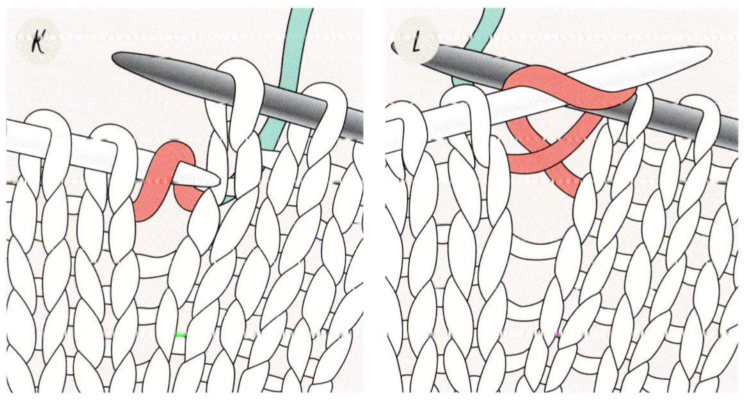

DECREASES

K2tog: Knit Two Stitches Together

Insert the tip of the right needle into the next two stitches from left to right and knit them as one stitch.

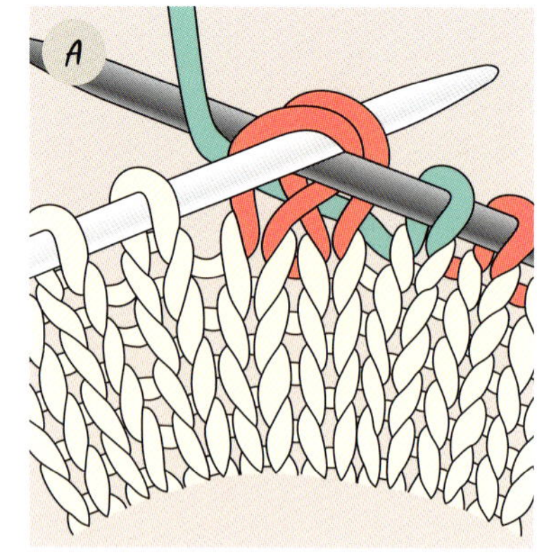

K2TOG IS A RIGHT-LEANING DECREASE, WHILE SSK IS A LEFT-LEANING DECREASE.

SSK: Slip, Slip, Knit

Keeping the yarn in back of the work, slip two stitches knitwise, one at a time (B) onto the right needle. Then knit the two stitches together through the back legs (C).

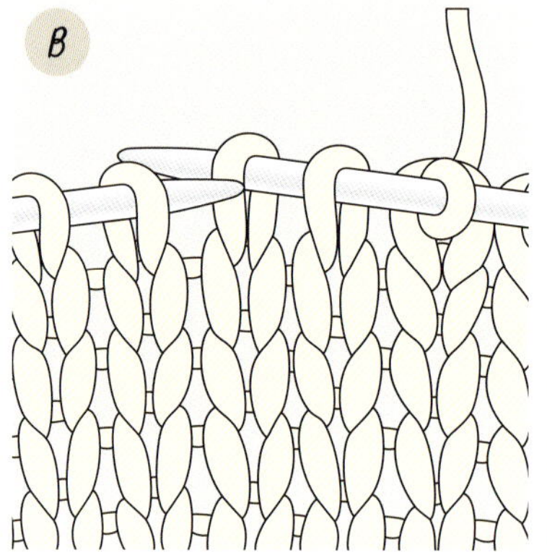

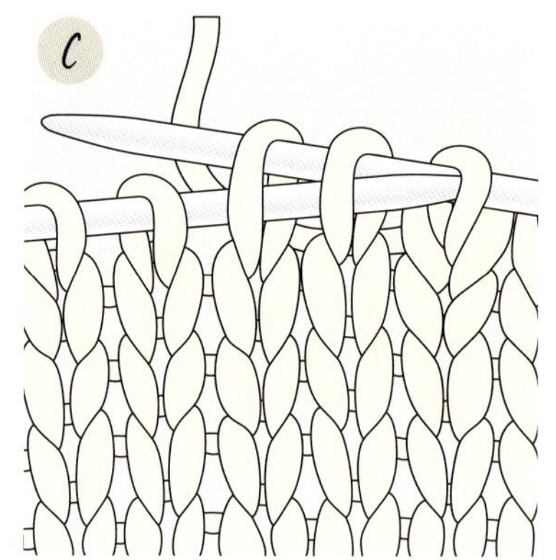

P2tog: Purl Two Stitches Together

Insert the tip of the right needle into the next two stitches from right to left and purl them as one stitch.

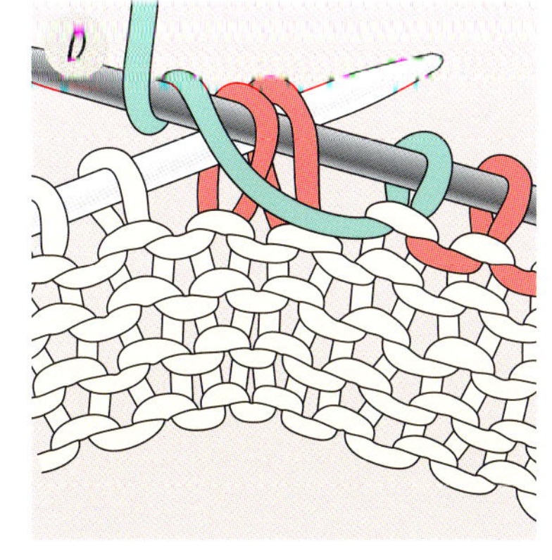

WHEN WORKING P2TOG ON THE WRONG SIDE OF THE FABRIC, THIS MATCHES THE LEAN OF A K2TOG.

SSP: Slip, Slip, Purl

Keeping the yarn in front of the work, slip two stitches knitwise, one at a time onto the right needle (E). Return the stitches to the left needle keeping them twisted (F). Then purl the two stitches together through the back legs (G).

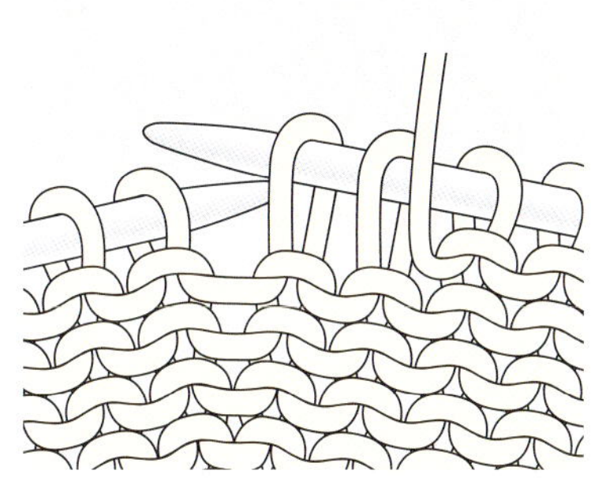

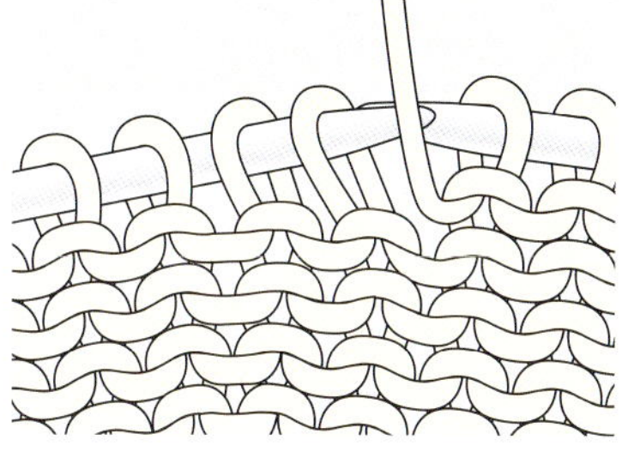

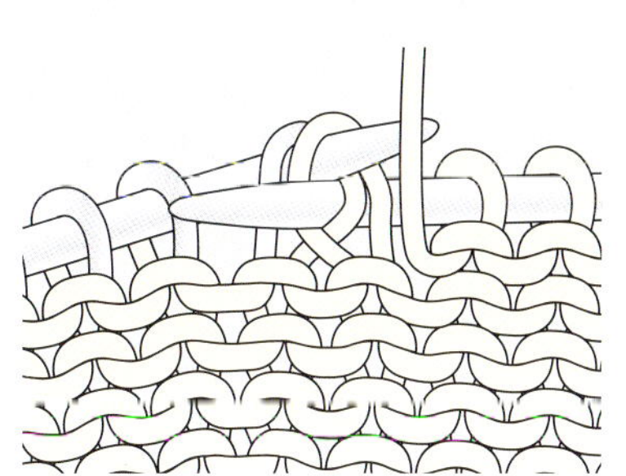

IT'S IMPORTANT TO SLIP THE STITCHES AS INSTRUCTED SO THE RESULTING DECREASE LEANS THE CORRECT WAY.

You're Ready

Dear Sock Knitters,

Yes, you are a sock knitter now! We have come to the end of the book but not the end of your sock knitting journey. This is just the beginning. Knit as many socks as you can, try as many heels as you can, knit them top down, toe up, and often.

I have always said on my YouTube channel and at my in-person classes, socks are the perfect canvas to practice and try out almost any knitting technique. The sky is the limit and the possibilities are endless.

Sock knitting is about experimentation. There may be times when it is necessary to rip out a portion or (gasp) all of your sock but never think of it as time wasted. You have used the knitting time to learn something new, figure out a problem, or gain insight toward a better fit. Any time spent sock knitting is worth it.

I hope this book has given you the confidence and strong foundation of understanding to tackle any sock knitting pattern and has answered your basic sock knitting questions. Most of all I hope it has taken the worry and fear out of sock knitting and replaced it with excitement, curiosity, and a deep love of socks!

Enjoy the journey, my friends!

Happy Sock Knitting,

Denise

EarthtonesGirl

About The Author

Denise DeSantis has been knitting for over 25 years but it wasn't until she started teaching sock knitting that she realized something was wrong. Sock knitting was considered hard, scary, and not for beginner knitters. A yarn shop owner even told her once, why knit socks when you can buy them. In that moment the challenge was accepted and the seed was planted.

Fast forward to 2020 when she began her No Fear Sock Knitting course on YouTube and started to teach knitters that with explanation, understanding, and practice, anyone could knit a pair of socks and enjoy the process from start to finish without the fear.

Before sock knitting, Denise was a massage therapist and labor support doula. She first fell in love with fiber at the age of eight when a friend taught her to crochet, which led to weekly trips to Woolworth to explore the yarn aisle. Yes, she is that old! Today, she lives in Westchester, NY, with her husband and two children, who step over weekly yarn deliveriess left at the front door.

She also loves audiobooks, tea, and quiet time with family and friends, all while sock knitting of course. Denise's passion to share her love of sock knitting is seen in every page of this book and her sincere wish is to spread that passion and a sense of fearlessness to as many knitters as possible.

Denise is known as EarthtonesGirl across social media platforms, including her YouTube channel, Instagram, and Ravelry. She also has a website where patterns and other knitting related items can be purchased.

YouTube: www.youtube.com/c/earthtonesgirlpodcast

Instagram: www.instagram.com/earthtonesgirl

Website: www.earthtonesgirl.com

Ravelry: www.ravelry.com/people/Earthtonesgirl

Acknowledgments

This book is the bucket list item I never knew I always wanted to achieve. Writing a book wasn't even on my list before Sarah C of David and Charles approached me with the idea. Thank you for seeing the potential and believing in my ability to achieve this huge goal. Thank you to the David and Charles team especially Victoria A and Sam S. To Tricia G, my tech editor, I don't have enough words to thank you for your guidance, support, and patience, and for helping me find the right words. To Karen P, my photographer, who sang along with me to the Indigo Girls and made my hands look beautiful.

To my husband for picking up as much of the day-to-day life stuff as he could so I could have the time to write and knit and bring this book to life. To my babies who I love more than yarn! To my friends, who listened and never got tired of listening. And to my May-May who would have cheered me on the loudest even though she would not have understood a word.

And thank you to everyone who bought my book, to all the knitters who learned to knit socks with me and shared their excitement, and to all the members of my online community, your support and encouragement mean the world to me!!

Suppliers

A huge thank you to all of the yarn dyers featured in this book. It was a pleasure working with your beautiful yarn.

KNOTTY PINE FIBER CO.

Instagram: @knottypinefiberco

Website: www.knottypinefiberco.com

LEGACY FIBER ARTZ

Instagram: @legacyfiberartz

Website: www.legacyfiberartz.com

MARIANATED YARNS

Instagram: @marianatedyarns

Website: www.marianatedyarns.com

MITCHELL'S CREATIONS

Instagram: @mitchellscfiberarts

Website: www.mitchellscreations.com

MUST STASH YARN

Instagram: @muststashyarn

Website: www.muststashshop.com

OPAL SOCK YARN

Available at your local or online yarn store

THE COZY KNITTER

Instagram: @thecozyknitter

Website: www.thecozyknitter.com/en-us

TINY HUMAN KNITS

Instagram: @tinyhumanknits

Website: www.etsy.com/shop/tinyhumanknits

WOOLENS AND NOSH

Instagram: @woolensandnosh

Website: www.woolensandnosh.com

Index

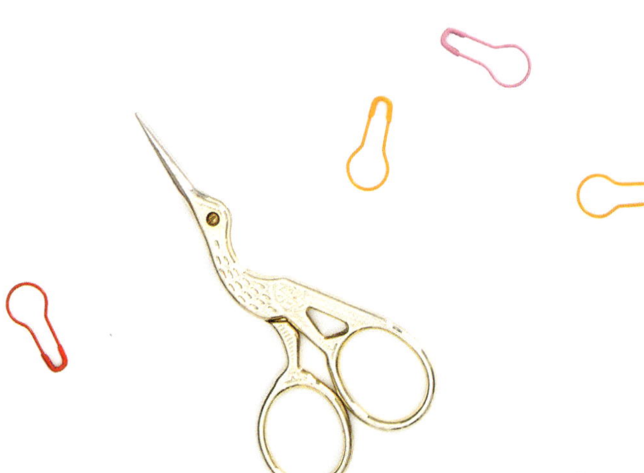

A DAVID AND CHARLES BOOK
© David and Charles, Ltd 2025

David and Charles is an imprint of David and Charles, Ltd
Suite A, Tourism House, Pynes Hill, Exeter, EX2 5WS

EU GPSR Authorised Representative:
Logos Europe, 9 rue Nicolas Poussin, 17000,
La Rochelle, France
Email: Contact@logoseurope.eu

Text and Designs © Denise DeSantis 2025
Layout and Photography © David and Charles, Ltd 2025

First published in the UK and USA in 2025

Denise DeSantis has asserted her right to be identified as author of this work in accordance with the Copyright, Designs and Patents Act, 1988.

All rights reserved. No part of this publication may be reproduced in any form or by any means, electronic or mechanical, by photocopying, recording or otherwise, without prior permission in writing from the publisher.

No part of this publication may be used or reproduced in any manner for the purpose of training artificial intelligence technologies or systems without permission from David and Charles Ltd.

Readers are permitted to reproduce any of the designs in this book for their personal use and without the prior permission of the publisher. However, the designs in this book are copyright and must not be reproduced for resale.

The author and publisher have made every effort to ensure that all the instructions in the book are accurate and safe, and therefore cannot accept liability for any resulting injury, damage or loss to persons or property, however it may arise.

Names of manufacturers and product ranges are provided for the information of readers, with no intention to infringe copyright or trademarks.

A catalogue record for this book is available from the British Library.

ISBN-13: 9781446315231 paperback
ISBN-13: 9781446315255 EPUB

This book has been printed on paper from approved suppliers and made from pulp from sustainable sources.

Printed in Bosnia and Herzegovina by GPS for:
David and Charles, Ltd
Suite A, Tourism House, Pynes Hill, Exeter, EX2 5WS

10 9 8 7 6 5 4 3

Publishing Director: Ame Verso
Publishing Manager: Jeni Chown
Senior Commissioning Editor: Sarah Callard
Editor: Victoria Allen
Project Editor: Tricia Gilbert
Art Direction and Design: Sam Staddon
Pre-press Designer: Susan Reansbury
Illustrations: Kuo Kang Chen
Photography: Jason Jenkins and Karen Pearson
Production Manager: Beverley Richardson

David and Charles publishes high-quality books on a wide range of subjects. For more information visit www.davidandcharles.com.

Share your makes with us on social media using #dandcbooks and follow us on Facebook and Instagram by searching for @dandcbooks.

Layout of the digital edition of this book may vary depending on reader hardware and display settings.